Marie L. Hoskins
Sibylle Artz
Editors

Working Relationally with Girls: Complex Lives/ Complex Identities

Working Relationally with Girls: Complex Lives/Complex Identities has been co-published simultaneously as *Child & Youth Services*, Volume 26, Number 2 2004.

Pre-publication
REVIEWS,
COMMENTARIES,
EVALUATIONS . . .

"Bringing together both reports of original research findings and reviews of the existing literature, the authors provide a rich understanding of how young women's gender identity is shaped by the intersection of their relational orientation and environmental forces existing in the lifespace. A major contribution of this book is the explicit attention to the challenge of exploring what is unique and individual among young women while attempting to build theory that incorporates the impact of gender as a powerful social category that profoundly influences individuals' experiences."

Naomi B. Farber, PhD, MSW
Associate Professor, University of South Carolina School of Social Work

Working Relationally with Girls: Complex Lives/ Complex Identities

Working Relationally with Girls: Complex Lives/Complex Identities has been co-published simultaneously as *Child & Youth Services*, Volume 26, Number 2 2004.

Monographic Separates from *Child & Youth Services*

For additional information on these and other Haworth Press titles, including descriptions, tables of contents, reviews, and prices, use the QuickSearch catalog at http://www.HaworthPress.com.

Working Relationally with Girls: Complex Lives/Complex Indentities, edited by Marie L. Hoskins, PhD, and Sibylle Artz, PhD (Vol. 26, No. 2, 2004). *"Bringing together both reports of original research findings and reviews of the existing literature, the authors provide a rich understanding of how young women's gender identity is shaped by the intersection of their relational orientation and environmental forces existing in the lifespace. A major contribution of this book is the explicit attention to the challenge of exploring what is unique and individual among young women while attempting to build theory that incorporates the impact of gender as a powerful social category that profoundly influences individuals' experiences."* (Naomi B. Farber, PhD, MSW, Associate Professor, University of South Carolina School of Social Work)

Themes and Stories in Youthwork Practice, edited by Mark Krueger (Vol. 26, No. 1, 2004). *"If you ever wanted to know what youth care work is, you should read this book. If you ever wondered what it can be, you should read it again. Useful to the practitioner, student, or teacher interested in discovering the depth of this work, this book offers a refreshing perspective from the traditional control and authority approaches so common in our field. It presents youth work as a living, vibrant, and personal experience of discovery for the youth and the worker. If you don't read it you are missing something important in your own education and development. It defines the possibilities of the field. In an eloquent and lyrical fashion, Krueger and his associates lead us through the experience that is youth work. This book is not for the superficial. It is for those who are truly interested in exploring the depth of this experience that we call youth work."* (Thom Garfat, PhD, Co-editor of CYC-Net International *and* Relational Child and Youth Care Practice; *Editor of* A Child and Youth Care Approach to Working with Families)

A Child and Youth Care Approach to Working with Families, edited by Thom Garfat, PhD (Vol. 25, No. 1/2, 2003). *"From ethics to data, from activities to support groups, from frontline to being in family homes–it's all here."* (Karl W. Gompf, BSc, MA, Consultant in Child and Youth Care, Red River College, Winnipeg, Manitoba, Canada)

Pain, Normality, and the Struggle for Congruence: Reinterpreting Residental Care for Children and Youth, James P. Anglin (Vol. 24, No. 1/2, 2002). *"Residential care practitioners, planners, and researchers will find much of value in this richly detailed monograph. Dr. Anglin's work adds considerably to our understanding of the residential care milieu as a crucible for change, as well as a scaffolding of support that transects community, child, and family."* (James Whitaker, PhD, Professor of Social Work, The University of Washington, Seattle)

Residential Child Care Staff Selection: Choose with Care, Meredith Kiraly (Vol. 23, No. 1/2, 2001). *"Meredith Kiraly is to be congratulated.... A lucid, readable book that presents the fruits of international experience and research relevant to the assessment and selection of child care workers, and which does so in a way that leads to practical strategies for achieving improvements in this important field. This book should be read by anyone responsible for selection into child care roles."* (Clive Fletcher, PhD, FBPsS, Emeritus Professor of Occupational Psychology, Goldsmiths' College, University of London; Managing Director, Personnel Assessment Limited)

Innovative Approaches in Working with Children and Youth: New Lessons from the Kibbutz, edited by Yuval Dror (Vol. 22, No. 1/2, 2001). *"Excellent.... Offers rich descriptions of Israel's varied and sustained efforts to use the educational and social life of the kibbutz to supply emotional and intellectual support for youngsters with a variety of special needs. An excellent supplement to any education course that explores approaches to serving disadvantaged children at risk of failing both academically and in terms of becoming contributing members of society."* (Steve Jacobson, PhD, Professor, Department of Educational Leadership and Policy, University of Buffalo, New York)

Working with Children on the Streets of Brazil: Politics and Practice, Walter de Oliveira, PhD (Vol. 21, No. 1/2, 2000). Working with Children on the Streets of Brazil *is both a scholarly work on the phenomenon of homeless children and a rousing call to action that will remind you of the reasons you chose to work in social services.*

Intergenerational Programs: Understanding What We Have Created, Valerie S. Kuehne, PhD (Vol. 20, No. 1/2, 1999).

Caring on the Streets: A Study of Detached Youthworkers, Jacquelyn Kay Thompson (Vol. 19, No. 2, 1999).

Boarding Schools at the Crossroads of Change: The Influence of Residential Education Institutions on National and Societal Development, Yitzhak Kashti (Vol. 19, No. 1, 1998). *"This book is an essential, applicable historical reference for those interested in positively molding the social future of the world's troubled youth." (Juvenile and Family Court Journal)*

The Occupational Experience of Residential Child and Youth Care Workers: Caring and Its Discontents, edited by Mordecai Arieli, PhD (Vol. 18, No. 2, 1997). *"Introduces the social reality of residential child and youth care as viewed by care workers, examining the problem of tension between workers and residents and how workers cope with stress." (Book News, Inc.)*

The Anthropology of Child and Youth Care Work, edited by Rivka A. Eisikovits, PhD (Vol. 18, No. 1, 1996). *"A fascinating combination of rich ethnographies from the occupational field of residential child and youth care and the challenging social paradigm of cultural perspective." (Mordecai Arieli, PhD, Senior Teacher, Educational Policy and Organization Department, Tel-Aviv University, Israel)*

Travels in the Trench Between Child Welfare Theory and Practice: A Case Study of Failed Promises and Prospects for Renewal, George Thomas, PhD, MSW (Vol. 17, No. 1/2, 1994). *"Thomas musters enough research and common sense to blow any proponent out of the water. . . . Here is a person of real integrity, speaking the sort of truth that makes self-serving administrators and governments quail." (Australian New Zealand Journal of Family Therapy)*

Negotiating Positive Identity in a Group Care Community: Reclaiming Uprooted Youth, Zvi Levy (Vol. 16, No. 2, 1993). *"This book will interest theoreticians, practitioners, and policymakers in child and youth care, teachers, and rehabilitation counselors. Recommended for academic and health science center library collections." (Academic Library Book Review)*

Information Systems in Child, Youth, and Family Agencies: Planning, Implementation, and Service Enhancement, edited by Anthony J. Grasso, DSW, and Irwin Epstein, PhD (Vol. 16, No. 1, 1993). *"Valuable to anyone interested in the design and the implementation of a Management Information System (MIS) in a social service agency. . ." (John G. Orme, PhD, Associate Professor, College of Social Work, University of Tennessee)*

Assessing Child Maltreatment Reports: The Problem of False Allegations, edited by Michael Robin, MPH, ACSW (Vol. 15, No. 2, 1991). *"A thoughtful contribution to the public debate about how to fix the beleaguered system . . . It should also be required reading in courses in child welfare." (Science Books & Films)*

People Care in Institutions: A Conceptual Schema and Its Application, edited by Yochanan Wozner, DSW (Vol. 14, No. 2, 1990). *"Provides ample information by which the effectiveness of internats and the life of staff and internees can be improved." (Residential Treatment for Children & Youth)*

Being in Child Care: A Journey Into Self, edited by Gerry Fewster, PhD (Vol. 14, No. 2, 1990). *"Evocative and provocative. Reading this absolutely compelling work provides a transformational experience in which one finds oneself alternately joyful, angry, puzzled, illuminated, warmed, chilled." (Karen VanderVen, PhD, Professor, Program in Child Development and Child Care, School of Social Work, University of Pittsburgh)*

Homeless Children: The Watchers and the Waiters, edited by Nancy Boxill, PhD (Vol. 14, No. 1, 1990). *"Fill[s] a gap in the popular and professional literature on homelessness. . . . Policymakers, program developers, and social welfare practitioners will find it particularly useful." (Science Books & Films)*

Perspectives in Professional Child and Youth Care, edited by James P. Anglin, MSW, Carey J. Denholm, PhD, Roy V. Ferguson, PhD, and Alan R. Pence, PhD (Vol. 13, No. 1/2, 1990). *"Reinforced by empirical research and clear conceptual thinking, as well as the recognition of the relevance of personal transformation in understanding quality care." (Virginia Child Protection Newsletter)*

Working Relationally with Girls: Complex Lives/ Complex Identities

Marie L. Hoskins
Sibylle Artz
Editors

Working Relationally with Girls: Complex Lives/Complex Identities has been co-published simultaneously as *Child & Youth Services*, Volume 26, Number 2 2004.

The Haworth Press, Inc.

New York • London • Victoria (AU)
www.HaworthPress.com

Working Relationally with Girls: Complex Lives/Complex Identities has been co-published simultaneously as *Child & Youth Services*™, Volume 26, Number 2 2004.

The development, preparation, and publication of this work has been undertaken with great care. However, the publisher, employees, editors, and agents of The Haworth Press and all imprints of The Haworth Press, Inc. including The Haworth Medical Press® and Pharmaceutical Products Press®, are not responsible for any errors contained herein or for consequences that may ensue from use of materials or information contained in this work. Opinions expressed by the author(s) are not necessarily those of The Haworth Press, Inc. With regard to case studies, identities and circumstances of individuals discussed herein have been changed to protect confidentiality. Any resemblance to actual persons, living or dead, is entirely coincidental.

The Haworth Press, Inc., 10 Alice Street, Binghamton, NY 13904-1580 USA

Cover design by Kerry E. Mack

Library of Congress Cataloging-in-Publication Data
Hoskins, Marie L.
Working relationally with girls : complex lives–complex identities / Marie L. Hoskins, Sibylle Artz, editors.
      p. cm.
    "[Also] published . . . as Child & youth services, volume 26, number 2, 2004."
    Includes bibliographical references and index.
    ISBN-13: 978-0-7890-2992-8 (hard cover : alk. paper)
    ISBN-10: 0-7890-2992-8 (hard cover : alk. paper)
    ISBN-13: 978-0-7890-2993-5 (soft cover : alk. paper)
    ISBN-10: 0-7890-2993-6 (soft cover : alk. paper)
       1. Teenage girls–Psychology. 2. Gender identity. 3. Identity (Psychology) in adolescence. 4. Teenage girls–Social conditions. 5. Social work with youth. I. Artz, Sibylle, 1949- II. Title.
HQ798.H67 2005
305.235′2–dc22
                                                            2005010555

Indexing, Abstracting & Website/Internet Coverage

This section provides you with a list of major indexing & abstracting services and other tools for bibliographic access. That is to say, each service began covering this periodical during the year noted in the right column. Most Websites which are listed below have indicated that they will either post, disseminate, compile, archive, cite or alert their own Website users with research-based content from this work. (This list is as current as the copyright date of this publication.)

(continued)

(continued)

*Special Bibliographic Notes related to special journal issues
(separates) and indexing/abstracting:*

- indexing/abstracting services in this list will also cover material in any "separate" that is co-published simultaneously with Haworth's special thematic journal issue or DocuSerial. Indexing/abstracting usually covers material at the article/chapter level.
- monographic co-editions are intended for either non-subscribers or libraries which intend to purchase a second copy for their circulating collections.
- monographic co-editions are reported to all jobbers/wholesalers/approval plans. The source journal is listed as the "series" to assist the prevention of duplicate purchasing in the same manner utilized for books-in-series.
- to facilitate user/access services all indexing/abstracting services are encouraged to utilize the co-indexing entry note indicated at the bottom of the first page of each article/chapter/contribution.
- this is intended to assist a library user of any reference tool (whether print, electronic, online, or CD-ROM) to locate the monographic version if the library has purchased this version but not a subscription to the source journal.
- individual articles/chapters in any Haworth publication are also available through the Haworth Document Delivery Service (HDDS).

ABOUT THE EDITORS

Dr. Marie L. Hoskins, Associate Professor in the School of Child and Youth Care at the University of Victoria, has a range of practice experiences including working in group homes, residential care, and working in the area of eating disorders and addictions. Her teaching has focused on the area of human change processes, the intersections between philosophical and theoretical approaches to change, and qualitative research methodologies. Her research interests focus on the social construction of knowledge, how cultural discourses impact identities, and youth popular culture.

During the past five years, Dr. Hoskins has been involved in two major research projects, entitled *The Experience of Mothering Daughters with Eating Disorders* and *Diversity: The Experience of Change When Shifting Worldviews.* Currently she is the principal investigator on a Social Sciences and Humanities Research Council Grant that explores adolescent girls' narratives of identity in relation to popular culture while recovering from an eating disorder.

Dr. Hoskins has published in a wide variety of journals such as the *Journal of Constructivist Psychology, Constructivism and the Human Sciences, the International Journal of Women's Health, the Child and Youth Care Forum, Qualitative Inquiry,* and the *Canadian Journal of Counselling.* She is a member of the International Advisory Committee for Constructivism and the Human Sciences, the Centre for Youth and Society and the Centre for Addictions at the University of Victoria.

Dr. Sibylle Artz, Full Professor, is the Director of the School of Child and Youth Care at the University of Victoria. She has more than twenty-one years of front-line experience with children, youth and their families. Her research interests include the challenges of practice in Child and Youth Care, the constructive use of emotion in direct practice, emotion and conflict, violence and homelessness and youth violence, with a specific focus on violence among adolescent females. In

January of 1994, *Feeling as a Way of Knowing: A Practical Guide to Working with Emotional Experience,* her first book, was published by Trifolium Books. In 1998, *Sex, Power and the Violent School Girl,* her second book, was released by Trifolium Books and Teachers College Press. Also in 1998, she was chosen as Academic of the Year by the Confederation of University Faculty Associations of British Columbia. In 2004, she received the McCreary Youth Foundation Award of Distinction for Research. Together with Dr. Douglas Magnuson, Northern Iowa University, she co-edits the international journal *Child and Youth Care Forum.*

Working Relationally with Girls: Complex Lives/ Complex Identities

CONTENTS

Introduction

Local and Global Realities: Theorizing Gender Relations

Marie L. Hoskins
Sibylle Artz

Writing a book about working with girls' relational dilemmas, whether focused on intrapersonal tensions, interpersonal conflict, or difficulties due to relationships with societal rules, norms, or media, is not an easy task. For every statement about the experience of being a girl in today's society, exceptions confound attempts to present an overall unified theory of experience. "Yes, but . . ." is a valid response to any universal knowledge claims. Postmodern discourse and scholarship have alerted us to the danger of making widespread knowledge claims that gloss over and sometimes negate individual differences. Given the acknowledged limitations, we struggle to build a viable framework from which to proceed with our work with girls.

Not surprisingly, we have found that sharing knowledge regarding gender power relations can be challenging on many levels. Although we wholeheartedly agree that girls can benefit from becoming more aware

Marie L. Hoskins, PhD, is Associate Professor, and Sibylle Artz, PhD, is Professor and Director, School of Child and Youth Care, Faculty of Human and Social Development, University of Victoria.

Address correspondence to: Dr. Marie L. Hoskins, School of Child and Youth Care, Faculty of Human and Social Development, University of Victoria, Box 1700, Victoria, BC, V8W 2Y2, Canada (E-mail: mhoskins@uvic.ca).

[Haworth co-indexing entry note]: "Introduction: Local and Global Realities: Theorizing Gender Relations." Hoskins, Marie L., and Sibylle Artz. Co-published simultaneously in Child & Youth Services (The Haworth Press, Inc.) Vol. 26, No. 2, 2004, pp. 1-8; and: Working Relationally with Girls: Complex Lives/Complex Identities (ed: Marie L. Hoskins, and Sibylle Artz) The Haworth Press, Inc., 2004, pp. 1-8. Single or multiple copies of this article are available for a fee from The Haworth Document Delivery Service [1-800-HAWORTH, 9:00 a.m. - 5:00 p.m. (EST). E-mail address: docdelivery@haworthpress.com].

of discourses that restrict their choices, even a gentle and general discussion of the still widespread limitations placed on girls often reveals their desire to minimize the impact of oppression and gender on everyday experience. So often young women want to see themselves as no longer hindered and no longer oppressed while being equal and, at the same time, in no way threatening to males. Thus, ignorance of the issues becomes bliss and a way out of having to face what has yet to be done.

When it comes to understanding the subtle and not so subtle discursive practices (rules, norms, laws, policies, scripts, and so on) that shape girls' lives, there are several tensions that deserve mentioning. Given the complexity of constructing an identity amidst the multiple, contradictory, fragmented scripts that pervade North American culture, we believe that we need to be continuously mindful of how our theories are used when we work with girls. Thus, in order to more fully understand girls' relational difficulties, we need to understand how certain discourses have a constitutive effect on human experience and, in turn, identity. We begin this introductory article with our reflections on these kinds of difficulties in order to set the stage for the valuable syntheses of theory and practice presented in this edition.

CONCEPTUALIZING GENDERED IDENTITIES

For decades, feminist writers have been developing theories about what it means to live in a patriarchal society (see, for example, Bordo, 1993; Brumberg, 1997; Butler, 1990, 1993; de Beauvoir, 1974; Faludi, 1991; Gergen, 2001). What comes through in this vast body of literature is the difficulty of trying to develop a universal theory that has enough external validity to represent women's experience and, at the same time, allows for individual differences. Although the point that no individual woman can speak for *all* women has been repeatedly underscored, the issue of how to generalize enough to even presume to know how to work with girls remains a challenge.

Complicating the issue of generalization is what we now know from certain developmental theories about identity construction which, briefly stated, is that gender identities are never stable, singular, or created in isolation (Efran & Fauber, 1995; Gergen, 1991; Harre & Gillett, 1994; Mahoney, 1991, 2003; Taylor, 1989). Because we are highly relational beings, our evolving identities are always a reflection of active participation with our environments (Maturana & Varela, 1987). Such environments consist of networks of societal attitudes, rules, norms, values, policies, cultural artifacts, and our physical location–trees, rivers and so on–meaning that our physical and non-physical environments are also highly relational (Haraway, 1988; Harding, 1991). Despite our shared participation in any number of environmental spaces, gender does not have the same meaning in everyone's life.

It is possible to speak of gender as a social construct; however, given the way our societies are organized, gender is not infinitely variable or negotiable. Our social agreements and organizations have roles and rules that are shared and therefore place shared demands upon us. Not just any kind of gendered identity is possible. Despite the often rigid boundaries around gender, it is still useful to acknowledge that gender is not only a social construct but also a process of actively engendering oneself. People take up certain kinds of behaviors or scripts that are associated with a particular interpretation of gender. Gender is, of course, not the only or necessarily primary way to create one's identity. Categories such as ethnicity, socio-economic status, and sexual orientation also make up the intersections of self and other in the world.

The fact that societal rules for being a male or female are socially constructed does not make them any less real. Within the psychological literature, women's experience in the world is often expressed as fundamentally different from men's (see, for example, Belenky, Clinchy, Goldberger, & Tarule, 1986; Brown & Gilligan, 1992; Gergen, 2001; and several of the authors in this edition). Difference, however, is a contentious issue among feminist practitioners and researchers. Although many feminists draw attention to the subordinate position of women all across the globe to strengthen anti-sexist work, they are also aware that it is unethical to parallel women's conditions in developing countries with those in North America. Women of color also strongly protest when White women put all women's concerns in the same overflowing box (see, for example, hooks, 1981, 1984, 1994; Moraga & Anzaldua, 1983).

So how are we alike and how are we different? Or is this even the appropriate question when attempting to theorize gender and practice? Wolf (1994) points out the difficulties in these kinds of formulations when she argues that recognition of difference can be problematic when women are slotted into the category of "woman." Women, according to Wolf, have been recognized as *nothing but women* for too long. Problematizing this issue, she argues that,

The question of how to move beyond that specific, distorting type of recognition is problematic in part because there is not a clear, or a clearly desirable, separate cultural heritage by which to redefine and reinterpret what it is to have an identity as a woman. (p. 76)

How, then, is it possible to work with the construction of gender when there are so many differences in how gender categories are constructed and experienced? How can we theorize without essentializing women? If the role of theory is to guide our actions as practitioners, how can we use theories without imposing them on those we work with?

AWARENESS OF SOCIETAL STRUCTURES: UNDERSTANDING THE LIFESPACE

In order to understand oppression and, in turn, the experiences of those who are marginalized (in this case, women) it is important to have a basic understanding of the societal influences that shape identities. In many disciplines this often translates into knowledge of how policies and legislation affect people's lives.

Historically, within the discipline of child and youth development and care, there is general agreement that what is most essential is understanding the lifespace of the children and youth we work with (see Hoskins & Mathieson, this volume, for a review of the literature). What is particularly challenging about this kind of contextually based knowledge is that such spaces cannot be understood in objective and factual ways. In other words, we cannot assume that we know how individuals make meaning of certain aspects of their context and how this, in turn, contributes to an individual's lifespace.

Hence, lifespace needs to include in its definition the idea that people are actively engaged in constructing meanings from and within their surroundings. Not just any meanings and interpretations are acceptable or viable particularly when they violate laws, professional codes of conduct, and certain societal norms. But apart from criminal activity and obvious ethical violations, if each individual is the interpreter and creator of his or her lifespace, then who are we to correct such interpretations? In particular, how are we to justify our attempts to provide our own insights about gender relations? This is where interventions become particularly challenging. Child and youth care researchers and practitioners have specific knowledge (developmental theories, social theory, policy, human rights legislation, and so on), and therefore it could be argued that we are in knowledgeable positions to educate girls about how macro-systems influence individual experiences. Yet, if each person has the capacity to be an active participant in the interpretation of experience, how can we respectfully intervene without imposing our own worldviews on children and youth, particularly when it comes to gender relations?

Although one could argue that adults' responsibility is to guide and teach, when it comes to gender relations such knowledge is fluid, contradictory, contextual, and under constant revision. Are girls victims of discursive practices or are they ultimately free to choose? Are their choices limitless or constrained? Is the feminist movement a great success or a dismal failure? Given these polarized positions, how do we negotiate our way through the complexities of certain gender relations and positions?

This brings us to the issue raised at the beginning of this introduction: ignorance may be bliss and the subsequent challenges that arise from this attitude towards oppression and women in particular need to be addressed. During the last few years we have found that while teaching feminist theory in our undergraduate courses, we are often met with resistance and, sometimes, indifference. It appears that feminist ideals are not openly embraced, particularly by younger female students. In conversations with other colleagues from Canada and the U.S., this seems to be a rather common reaction among students. There could be several explanations for these reactions: media backlash against feminism, an inclination to return to fundamental values riding on a wave of neo-conservatism, especially in the U.S., or divisiveness among various feminist perspectives.

What this signals for us is the difficulty that arises when attempting to draw attention to the complex relationship between the social construction of gender and everyday lived experience. Discussing gender relations with our students, clients, and research participants, therefore, becomes challenging for several reasons. Particularly challenging is that, invariably, increased gender consciousness requires a change of some kind on the part of the individual. Girls often describe being caught in a double bind when they challenge sexist attitudes and behaviors. Another aspect of the ignorance is bliss theme is that many young women want to be able to identify with social constructions of what it means to be "feminine," not necessarily feminist. Often this means identifying with hyper-feminine characteristics such as being cooperative, nice, agreeable, sexually appealing, and so on, so much so that when it comes to challenging the status quo girls also find themselves challenging their own "good girl" images. In our classrooms, students often state that they do not want to be angry, assertive, disruptive, and that, above all, they do not want to be seen as hating men, characteristics and approaches they describe as associated with feminism.

PROCESSES OF CHANGE: INDIVIDUAL AND SYSTEMIC

Although periods of continuity and discontinuity are inherent fluctuations of human experience and are considered to be essential for growth and development, knowledge of such processes does not alleviate the discomfort associated with individual and systemic change. The same is true for the desire to name difficulties so that they can be regarded in a different way. Even when people are acutely aware of power relations that inhibit choice in their lives, this does not mean that articulating such processes will lessen their impact. Consciousness-raising is only one part of the complex process of change. For practitioners, it is difficult to work closely with clients, to engage with the intricacies of their problematic issues, while also keeping in mind the meta-structures that may have created the difficulties in the first place. Deeply listening to a person's description of experience often requires practitioners to "stay in the moment" instead of thinking structurally. This moving back and forth between meta-theories of gender relations, while listening carefully to clients' interpretations of their life experiences, requires advanced skills and a high level of awareness of one's beliefs about gender and girls.

When considering change on the part of clients, practitioners need to have some ideas, perhaps even working models, about how change takes place and what constitutes an actual change. If we intend to take gender into account, and we believe that there are definite gender differences with regard to how people make changes, we also need to include in our models and ideas gender specific markers. In our various research projects over the years, it has become increasingly apparent to us that girls *do* have critical insight about how things work within patriarchal societies and how girls and women are expected to fit into these social structures and strictures. They are able to describe situations in their schools and within their families where inequities occur but are also willing to accept that "boys will just be boys." They seem to be inclined to succumb to the ways things are because they have always been that way. "It's tradition," some girls explain to us and, regretfully from our perspective, seem willing to engage in rituals of self-denigration while readily exonerating males from sexist comments and actions.

In summary, there are definite tensions that exist when trying to work in the intersections between constructed, individual, and meta kinds of knowledge found in broad systems of thought such as critical theory, poststructural thinking, and feminist theory while at the same time dealing with everyday life and the lived experiences of real people trying to get by. We believe that what is most needed are creative and effective ideas for linking individual experience with more global, universal experiences of women in all of their diversity and complexities. There is great wisdom in what Shields refers to as "filigrees of well-spun theory" (p. 178), but these filigrees need to be carefully mixed with the unique everyday realities of girls' lives.

The subtle and not so subtle tensions that we have outlined encourage us to carry on in thoughtful and reflective ways as we are called to work relationally with girls. In this book, such tensions have become fruitful catalysts for moving forward and imagining improved lifespaces for girls. While the chapters in this book address many of the tensions briefly discussed above, they also offer practical suggestions for improving the ways in which we work with girls' dilemmas. Each takes a particular orientation to the construction of gender resulting in a rich and diverse collection of theoretical and practical ideas that are applicable to both research and practice. It is with great pleasure that we present this volume of selected chapters on how to work in the complex intersections of gendered identities.

REFERENCES

de Beauvoir, S. (1974). *The second sex* (2nd ed.). New York: Vintage Press.
Belenky, M., Clinchy, B., Goldberger, N., & Tarule, J. (1986). *Women's ways of knowing: The development of self, voice, and mind.* New York: Basic Books.
Bordo, S. (1993). *Unbearable weight: Feminism, western culture, and the body.* Berkeley, CA: University of California Press.
Brown, L. M., & Gilligan, C. (1992). *Meeting at the crossroads: Women's psychology and girls' development.* Cambridge, MA: Harvard University Press.
Brumberg, J. (1997). *The body project.* New York: Random House.
Butler, J. (1990). *Gender trouble: Feminism and the subversion of identity.* New York: Routledge.
Butler, J. (1993). *Bodies that matter: On the discursive limits of 'sex.'* New York: Routledge.

Efran, J., & Fauber, R. (1995). Radical constructivism: Questions and answers. In R. A. Neimeyer & M. J. Mahoney (Eds.), *Constructivism in psychotherapy* (pp. 275-304). Washington, DC: American Psychological Association.

Faludi, S. (1991). *Backlash: The undeclared war against American women*. New York: Crown.

Gergen, K. (1991). *The saturated self*. New York: Basic Books.

Gergen, M. (2001). *Feminist reconstructions in psychology: Narrative, gender, and performance*. Thousand Oaks, CA: Sage.

Haraway, D. (1988). *Simians, cyborgs, and women: The reinvention of nature*. New York: Routledge, Chapman, & Hall.

Harding, S. (1991). *Whose science? Whose knowledge? Thinking from women's lives*. New York: Cornell University Press.

Harre, R., & Gillett, G. (1994). *The discursive mind*. Thousand Oaks, CA: Sage.

hooks, b. (1981). *Ain't I a woman: Black women and feminism*. Boston, MA: South End Press.

hooks, b. (1984). *Feminist theory from margin to center*. Boston, MA: South End Press.

hooks, b. (1994). *Outlaw culture: Resisting representations*. New York: Routledge.

Mahoney, M. J. (1991). *Human change processes: The scientific foundations of psychotherapy*. New York: Basic Books.

Mahoney, M. J. (2003). *Constructive psychotherapy: A practical guide*. New York: The Guildford Press.

Maturana, H. R., & Varela, F. J. (1987). *The tree of knowledge*. London: Shambhala.

Moraga, C., & Anzaldua, G. (Eds.). (1983). *This bridge called my back: Writings by radical women of color* (2nd ed). New York: Kitchen Table, Women of Color Press.

Shields, C. (2002). *Unless: A novel*. Toronto, ON: Random House.

Taylor, C. (1989). *Sources of the self: The making of the modern identity*. Cambridge, MA: Harvard University Press.

Wolf, S. (1994). Comment. In C. Taylor (Ed.), *Multiculturalism* (pp. 75-86). Princeton, NJ: Princeton University Press.

Mothers' and Girls' Perspectives on Adolescent Sexuality

Marla Buchanan-Arvay
Patrice A. Keats

SUMMARY. A study of communication between mothers and daughters about mothers' sexual experience discloses mothers' and daughters' fears, concerns, and judgments about each other. In this study, 15 women, all mothers of girls, were interviewed about the history of their own sexual experience. Some of these women had chosen to share their personal experience with their daughters and some had not, although some were now willing. These stories were then shared with a group of girls, and then the girls were asked whether they would want to know about their own mothers' experience had they been similar. Like the mothers, some girls wanted to know and others did not. Reasons for

---

Marla Buchanan-Arvay, PhD, is Associate Professor, Department of Educational and Counselling Psychology, and Special Education, University of British Columbia. Patrice A. Keats, PhD, is Assistant Professor, Counselling Psychology Program, Simon Fraser University.

Address correspondence to: Dr. Marla Buchanan-Arvay, University of British Columbia, #280-2125 Main Mall, Scarfe Lib. Block, Vancouver, BC, V6T 1Z4, Canada (E-mail: marla.arvay@ubc.ca).

The authors wish to thank Kristine Einerson for her research assistance on this project.

This research was funded by a Humanities and Social Science Research Grant (HSS Grant) at the University of British Columbia. An earlier draft of the first phase of this research by the authors was published and is entitled: Arvay, M. J., & Keats, P. A. (2002). Opening Pandora's Box. *Journal for the Association for Research on Mothering* 4(1), 77-86.

[Haworth co-indexing entry note]: "Mothers' and Girls' Perspectives on Adolescent Sexuality." Buchanan-Arvay, Marla, and Patrice A. Keats. Co-published simultaneously in *Child & Youth Services* (The Haworth Press, Inc.) Vol. 26, No. 2, 2004, pp. 9-31; and: *Working Relationally with Girls: Complex Lives/Complex Identities* (ed: Marie L. Hoskins, and Sibylle Artz) The Haworth Press, Inc., 2004, pp. 9-31. Single or multiple copies of this article are available for a fee from The Haworth Document Delivery Service [1-800-HAWORTH, 9:00 a.m. - 5:00 p.m. (EST). E-mail address: docdelivery@haworthpress.com].

Digital Object Identifier: 10.1300/J024v26n02_02

sharing include helping protect daughters from mothers' own victimizing experience and opening up communication. Reasons for not sharing included violating boundaries between mothers and daughters and embarrassment. *[Article copies available for a fee from The Haworth Document Delivery Service: 1-800-HAWORTH. E-mail address: <docdelivery@haworthpress.com> Website: <http://www.HaworthPress.com> © 2004 by The Haworth Press, Inc. All rights reserved.]*

KEYWORDS. Sex education, parent communication, adolescent sexuality, mother-daughter relationships, women in families

INTRODUCTION

A Mother's Perspective

It was 1965 and I remember the "cruise" with my girlfriends in one of their father's cars down to the A & W Drive-in to get coney fries and a root beer, hoping to see my newest crush as we hopped around from car to car. We were comfortably safe, yet naive in our budding sexuality. We didn't have sex education in high school. Neither my mother nor any of my friends' mothers told us about intercourse or birth control. My best friend told me that her mother's sex advice was "Keep your skirt down and your legs crossed!" It was assumed that we wouldn't have sex until we were married. My mother never told me about menstruation; however, when she found the pads in the garbage she seemed hurt that I didn't tell her. I told her that I knew about it from my older sisters, but in truth it was my girlfriend who told me what it was and how to deal with it. This was the era in North America before HIV and AIDS. My girlfriends and I did not discuss the intimate details of our relationships; however, most of us were kissing and petting. I knew of only one girl who had intercourse, because she got pregnant in grade 12. If girls were having sex, it was a big secret.

A Daughter's Perspective

I turned 16 on the brink of the new millennium. I don't really remember learning about sex although my mother's story is that we went for a walk along the ocean and she told me about menstruation and sexual intercourse. She used clinical terms to describe the body parts and gave me a book to read, saying, "If you have any questions just ask me." She also told me that I could get birth control anytime that I felt I needed it. She said that she could come with me to the doctor or that I could make my own appointment. She never asked me directly if I was thinking about having sex or not and she never told me about STDs. We got that talk in school during co-ed life planning classes. We also had to practice putting a condom on plastic penises. It was hysterically funny. Most of my views about sex came from listening to a feminist rock star whose powerful lyrics helped to shape my ideas. Her lyrics expanded my ideas about sexual choices and sexual oppression. This was reinforced when, in grade ten, I started driving a girlfriend of mine to an all-girl Catholic school so that she could make out with another girl in the back of my car. The teachers and nuns restricted boys from the campus, but other girls were always welcome to visit or sleep over in the dorms on the weekends. I pondered during her coming out if I might be "bi." It was in grade eleven when I began what has now turned out to be a six-year relationship. I can see how I and my peers have more sexual freedom, more resources, and more sexual knowledge than our mothers. Although we have more access to sexual information, it hasn't freed us.

In these two stories from a 50-year-old mother and her 20-year-old daughter, the mother's and the daughter's descriptions of the roles their mothers played in their sex education miss personal aspects related to sexuality. Although they experienced their adolescence in different historical periods with different norms and expectations about women and sexuality, both women gleaned the majority of their sexual education from their peers. These two stories prompt the questions of how mothers and daughters perceive the generational differences regarding sexual experiences in adolescence and what mothers and daughters want to know or not know about each other's sexuality.

RESEARCHING MOTHER-DAUGHTER SEXUAL DISCOURSE

The literature is missing research about mothers telling their daughters about adolescent experiences of sexuality. We were curious about what mothers might be willing to share–or not share–with their adolescent daughters. We also wondered how their daughters would respond.

Feminist scholars researching women's identity issues (Daniluk, 1998; Flaake, 1994; Friedman, 1998; Hales, 1999; Kitzinger, 1995;

Martin, 1987; Northrup, 1998; Pipher, 1995; Rothman, 1989; Simanski, 1998; Walters, 1992; Wolf, 1997) noted that discourses on mothering and discourses on women's sexual identity development seem to be staged as competing discourses. These scholars argue that popular culture and cultural myths and norms regarding family values continue to censure the integration of women as both mothers and sexual beings. As Walters (1992) notes, there continues to be a struggle with this "double-bind discourse:" The mother-child relationship must have boundaries around sexuality and yet women are encouraged to claim their own sexual identity, an identity that is set outside of the maternal realm. Friedman (1998), for example, found that women perceive sexuality and mothering as mutually exclusive, emphasizing a nonsexual standard: the more sexual a woman is, the less she is seen as a good mother. She also found that participants' views on maintaining the separation between sexuality and motherhood were stronger among men than women and among younger parents versus older parents.

Although tensions between sexuality and maternity may be present in the communication between mothers and daughters in Western culture, culturally specific contexts also show mother-daughter communication as present but not always positive (O'Sullivan, Meyer-Bahlburg, & Watkins, 2001; Raffaelli & Green, 2003). There appears to be rising tensions as daughters develop towards their own sexual awareness. Other research demonstrates that both mothers and daughters may show specific styles or ways of approaching the topic of sexuality to compensate for these rising tensions (Rosenthal, Feldman, & Edwards, 1998; Yowell, 1997). For example, Rosenthal, Feldman, and Edwards (1998) constructed five types of styles (avoidant, reactive, opportunistic, child-initiated, and mutually interactive) in mothers' approaches to communicating about sexuality with their daughters. These styles appeared to affect how the conversations took place and what kinds of information were shared.

Several authors have reported that this division in women's identity between sexuality and maternity may impact communication about sexuality between mothers and daughters (Daniluk, 1998; DiIorio, Kelley, & Hockenberry-Eaton, 1999; Rosenthal & Feldman, 1999; Rosenthal, Feldman, & Edwards, 1998; Taris & Semin, 1997; Walters, 1992). However, research findings have been contradictory. For instance, Hutchinson and Cooney (1998), in their review of the literature, state, "Several studies have found no relationship between levels of parent-teen sexual communication and teen sexual activity . . . while other studies have found that teens with higher reported levels of communication with parents are less sexually active than others (p. 186).

In Rosenthal and Feldman's (1999) study, adolescents rated parental communication about sexuality as unimportant, and there was an overall perception that there was insufficient rather than excessive parental communication about sexuality. DiIorio, Kelly, and Hockenberry-Eaton (1999), in their predominantly African-American sample of 405 adolescents and 382 mothers, found that both male and female adolescents were more likely to discuss sex with their mothers than their fathers. They claim that adolescents who reported openly communicating with their mothers were more likely to have initiated sexual intercourse and to have conservative values. However, in O'Sullivan, Jaramillo, Moreau, and Meyer-Bahlburg's (1999) study with a sample of 110 Hispanic adolescent girls, communication with mothers about sexuality was not related to the adolescents' reported sexual behaviour. It appears that research findings regarding parental communication about sexuality and adolescent sexual behaviour are inconclusive. Further, few studies have investigated what mothers might or might not be willing to share with their daughters about their own adolescent sexual experiences and how daughters might respond to their mother's stories. In terms of mother-daughter relationships and communication about sexuality, what might this type of conversation reveal?

METHODOLOGY

This is a narrative study on mother/daughter communication regarding sexuality and sexual identity development from the perspective of a group of mothers and a group of adolescent females. Our aim was to explore conversations about adolescent sexuality from the viewpoints of mothers and daughters to further our understandings of generational differences. In our original research design, we anticipated interviewing 12 to 15 mothers and then hoped to have follow-up interviews with their adolescent daughters. However, not all the mothers in this study consented to have their daughters interviewed. Therefore, in the second stage of this study we interviewed 12 adolescent females who were not related to the mothers in the first part of the study. Each of the 12 adolescents read and responded to one of the mothers' narratives describing their adolescent sexuality experiences. This meant that each mother had their story responded to by an adolescent. The participants were reading and commenting on an unknown mother's story.

The study consisted of two distinct phases. Phase one focused on collecting and creating narratives of mothers' descriptions of their adolescent sexual experiences. Phase two focused on adolescent girls' reactions to the narratives. All participants in both phases were given pseudonyms to provide anonymity and protect confidentiality.

Participants in Phase One

Our group of mothers included a sample of 15 women between the ages of 38 and 57 (mean age of 50 years) who had adolescent daughters. Two mothers were First Nations, ten were white and grew up in Canada, and three women lived in other countries during their adolescent years: two from South Africa and one from Scotland. All participants were recruited through advertisements posted at two community centers, the local university, and through word-of-mouth.

Data Collection: The Interviews in Phase One

We interviewed the mothers in order to understand their perspectives on telling or not telling their sexual development stories to their own daughters, seeking to know what elements needed to exist for mothers to talk freely with their daughters about both personal and interpersonal issues. The women were invited to talk about their own adolescent sexual experiences in individual audiotaped, semi-structured interviews that ranged from 90 to 180 minutes in length. All of the women were interviewed in their homes.

After each mother described her sexual experiences during adolescence, she was asked if she had shared or had not shared this story with her adolescent daughter(s). If she had shared, she was asked how telling about her own adolescent sexual experiences had been received by her daughter(s). If she had not shared, we asked her to tell us more about her reasons for not sharing. Three participants stated that they had already shared some parts of their story with their daughters; the remaining 12 participants had not.

Analysis of the Data in Phase One

The transcripts were analyzed using a collaborative narrative method (Arvay, 2003) that included four separate readings of the transcripts: (a) reading for the content of the story (e.g., What is the story line? Is the story clear? What is the sequence of events in this story? Is further clarification needed?); (b) reading for the identity construction of the narrator (e.g., Who is telling this story? What is revealed about the protagonist in this story? How does she position herself in this text? What does she want us to know about her? What metaphors and other tropes does she use to narrate herself in this text?); (c) reading for the research questions and, finally, (d) a discursive reading for relations of power (e.g., Where does she use her voice and with what result? Where is she silenced or silencing herself? What is not said but implied? What discourses does she take up that either enhance or restrict her expression of her own sexuality? How does culture speak through this tale? What is at stake in this story?)

After the four readings of each interview were completed, we created a narrative account for each mother's transcript. We returned the narrative account to each mother requesting that they review their own account in order to make any desired changes to the content. Only three words were changed after the member check procedures were completed. These word replacements did not change the content or meaning of the story being told.

After the narratives were returned, we asked the mothers if they would be willing to share this written account with their own adolescent daughter(s). Of the 12 who had not yet shared their stories with their own daughter(s), only 4 stated that they would be willing to share the researchers' narrative account. At this point, 3 participants decided to drop out of the study for the following reasons: "I am not comfortable with people reading my story." "The story is too raw–I am embarrassed if others read it." "I don't want anyone to read it because it is too exposing–I am not ready to show this to anyone." This left us with 12 remaining mothers: Three who stated they had shared their narratives already, 4 who stated that they would be willing to share their stories, and 5 who were unwilling to share their stories with their own daughters.

FINDINGS

We present two prototype stories that reflect both sides of the mothers' debate–whether to share or not. The first participant, Betty, stated that she would *not be willing to share* this narrative with her daughter. Marley, the second participant, stated that she *would openly share* her story with her adolescent daughters without reservation. We present their stories first, followed by a discussion of key elements of all the mothers' stories. Finally, we will present the adolescent females' responses to the mothers' stories and a discussion of the implications of the findings for mother-daughter communication and female sexual identity development.

Betty's Narrative Account (Would Not Tell)

I grew up in a small village in Scotland with my older sister. Being raised in a rural environment, I was very present in my body and in the earth; I was part sheep. I specifically remember my dad coming home from the Second World War–a blonde, blue-eyed god. I experienced the magic of manhood–the magic thing of male power as he and his friends gathered in our home to sing and play the bagpipes. At the age of 7, my dad started his own business–a service station. It was a big thing to own land, moving away from the feudal system and, at that time, we moved into our own place above the service station. On moving day, my mother gave me this very important task–a dish of macaroni and cheese to carry to the new house. At 7, I discovered that I could grow up and be a woman. I could carry the food.

By the age of 9 my relationship with my father started to change. He told me I was too old for hugging and kissing. That was the end of the evening hug and kiss from my dad. I remember crying in my bedroom, knowing my dad heard me. I knew that he was sitting in the next room hardening his heart.

It was not until I was about 11 that I experienced anything sexual. My first great sexual experience was swinging on a rope swing in a tree. I had this great orgasmic experience. It was a big mystery. No one had ever told me anything and no one could possibly have experienced anything like this. Not knowing what it was that had happened, I tried to find ways to make it happen again. I did not make any sense of it nor did I speak to anyone about it. I just felt it.

About the same time that I had the experience in the tree, I started my first period and it was quite traumatic. Nobody had said anything about it to me. I was riding home on my bike and I saw blood on my green and white checkered dress. I did not know what it was. When I saw my mom, she said she should have told me about it since she was a nurse. She showed me how to use the belts and pads. They were awful things. At school there was one toilet and it was stone cold and dirty. I had to share it with hundreds of other children. There was no privacy to change your pad nor could you carry a pad to school. No one told me it was important to wash. In Scotland you were lucky to get a bath once a week. It was awful, awful, and grim. It was just so grim.

When I was 13, my sister and I went to another school, riding our bikes to the train to get to the school. There were many boys on the train and my sister told me to cover my knees, not to smile with my teeth showing, and things like that. My sister got the idea that sexuality was bad from my mom, who got it from my granny because my grandfather was a minister. It was clear that I was not to wear anything revealing, yet I never got this message directly from my mom. She spoke to my sister and then my sister passed it on to me. No one talked about sex. There was no sex education and girls did not talk about it with each other because we were rivals. We were only interested in the boys. It was so fun, the magic of boys.

The first kiss—oh happy days, happy days! It happened after a Sunday School party when a boy walked me home. It was magic and innocent—so innocent. We did not know anything. I did not know what a penis was. I could not have told a penis from a tree. I did not know that boys had them and I had never seen one. I was so innocent. I had never seen anyone naked.

There was a lot of kissing. When I was 14 there started to be fondling. I remember those intense feelings of romance and seeking relationships with boys. It really drove my whole adolescence. When I was 15, I fell for a boy really hard. I saw him everyday and there was a lot of kissing and touching but nothing genital. It was really innocent. It was all so connected with the landscape. When he broke up with me, I was heartbroken—it really cut deep. It was such a sweet relationship, so sweet. This was a beautiful first love.

After about a year, I trapped a guy. I snared the guy of my dreams. In that relationship, I had my own sense of deepening, my own sexuality. We went deeper into the sexual world, but still it was not intercourse. I remember intense feelings of sexual desire but I did not know what to do with it. There was a lot of touching but not in a genital way. There was never any talk of, "Should we have sex?" I just knew that I was not going to do that because it was just not done. I was afraid of getting pregnant. I still did not know that penises got erect, although I must have known about getting pregnant.

There was nothing about birth control at the time. No one talked about birth control. There was a sense of mystery about sex as something that happened when you got married. You did not have sex because you were not married and you waited until you were married to have sex. That was the cultural code. I believed that I would not have sex until I was married and whomever I had sex with was the person I would marry. When it did happen at age 22, it was a big mistake–such a mistake. I was not in love with him but I knew it was time to have sex. It was very disappointing. His penis penetrated me, but I was not going to feel anything. It was not safe to feel anything. After the rope swing, there was lots of masturbating going on, but I did not make the connection between that experience and sex with a man. I never knew it happened with boys. It was somehow separate.

Marley's Narrative Account (Would Tell)

I was born on Vancouver Island in 1941. I remember my mother telling me that I was lucky to have such shiny beautiful hair because it helped to make up for the fact that I was an ugly duckling. She threatened me if I didn't behave for grandma by saying she would take me to the men's barber shop where they would cut off my hair.

I was abandoned by my mother as a child and raised by my maternal grandmother. When I was 6 my grandma died and I moved next door to my grandma's kindly old friend and her husband–Granny and Grandpa M. He was a pedophile who molested me twice when I was 7. I felt confused, guilty, and ashamed of myself. Granny came home one day and caught him molesting me. She asked me, "Did that dirty old bugger touch you inside your underwear?" I said "yes" and then she took care of me and phoned my mother to say she couldn't keep me anymore.

Then I went to live in foster care where I learned that boys were favored over girls. I wished that I were a boy. When I was 11 years old my mother finally rescued me from the foster care and, for the first time in my life, I lived with my mother. She was remarried and we were going to have a home and be a family. I felt a sense of security and stability because I had a structured routine at home and I felt good.

I got my period at 11. I was so happy because some of my school chums had gotten theirs already. It made me feel like I belonged. I thought my mother would be happy for me, but she wasn't–instead she was furious. The first thing she said to me was, "Now we have really got problems!" She meant now I had the potential to become a pregnant teenager. You see, she became pregnant with me as a teenager so that incident burst my bubble. I knew that we weren't suddenly going to become magically close and have a special relationship. She didn't take the time to show me how to put the pad and belt together. She just angrily harnessed me into this strange foreign rig and left me there in the bathroom. I remember crying and not knowing how to change the pad. I developed pubic hair around the time I began my menses and I remember being aware of it especially when I was close to 16, anxiously wondering, "Oh my god! When will it stop growing? Is there no end to it?"

When I was about 13 or 14 years old, I became interested in boys and I remember living a double life. By day, I seemed so shy and innocent and by night daring and bold, stuffing my brassier with woolly gloves and heading out alone for the nearby ice rink. I wanted to have the biggest, most obvious boobs so that the older boys would notice me and ask me to skate with them. This is my first memory of wanting to be irresistibly sexy and desirable to men and wanting a man to kiss me and make love to me.

I finally got a best friend and we would go out and be bad and get into trouble together. We were the sluts of the school. My friend and I would go out streetwalking together, stroll up and down the main street all gussied up in linen suits, nylons, and high-heeled shoes, lots of makeup and tacky paper flowers stuck in our hair. We desperately wanted the boys in the cars to pick us up. Those boys never did pick us up, but we both got some sexual experience with this young cab driver who worked for a taxi service. He took me out one night and we necked and petted in his car. That was my first kiss. The next night he took my friend out and they did the same thing.

One night I went out streetwalking all by myself. I got all gussied up and snuck out of the window and went strolling down the highway. Two guys picked me up in their car and we drove around for a while just cruising and burning gas. I went back to their apartment and ended up having sexual intercourse with the driver of the car. God, I was such a tramp. When he was having sex with me it was not like being in my body. I felt so emotionally detached from the experience. I was passive and numb, like when I was molested by my Grandpa M. It was something being done to me. However, I felt older–like I was progressing somehow. I was hoping the boy would want me to be his girlfriend, but I never saw him again.

When I began grade 10, I was acutely aware of my reputation among my peers. I knew that I had better tidy up my act if I was to fit in and be accepted–and so I did. I ended up just hanging out with my classmates and doing normal teenage things. I went out with a boy for a month and we had sex but there was some respectability to it because he was my boyfriend. However, he dumped me after a month. It was about this same time that my stepfather started to be very cruel to me. He accused me of sleeping around, but I wasn't. I wanted to have a good reputation. My mother thought I was out of control too. This made me angry and I said to myself "Well, if that is what you think, then that is what I will be." I started staying out later, drinking more and becoming more promiscuous by flirting and petting with different guys. When I was 17, I finally had one steady boyfriend for a whole year. It made me happy to have a boyfriend and be a part of the crowd. I had sex with him maybe once every ten dates, which seemed to be the norm in those days.

When I graduated from high school, my stepfather gave my mother an ultimatum: either she could live with him or me. Obviously, she chose him. There was never any hope for me with my mom. I felt so much hostility and resentment toward her. I mean, her obligation to take care of me was over, so she didn't need to even think twice about it. Looking back now, I sort of regret I didn't appreciate Mother's position more; I mean, objectively speaking, it was normal that she'd choose to live with her husband rather than her grown child who was old enough to move out on her own anyway.

Mothers Who Chose Not to Share

Five of the participants in this study (plus the 3 who dropped out of the study) chose not to share their early sexual experiences with their daughters. Their reasons for not sharing can be summarized briefly as maintaining the assumption that their daughters did not really want to know about this story. They felt that it was embarrassing for both themselves and their daughters. One stated that it was not appropriate: "I think my personal experience is private. I do not think that my privacy should be invaded because I am a parent. I do not give my daughter information about me that she may not want to know. It is about respect and dignity–for her and me." Three stated that they feared being rejected for seeming to be "over-sexed." It left them feeling "vulnerable" and "insecure" and worried it would "alter" their daughter's image of them "in a negative way."

Mothers Who Chose to Share

Three participants said that they already had shared their story with their daughter(s).

Anne: This study has been so incredibly useful to me at a time when I was struggling with my daughter's emerging sexuality. I shared the story with her. It opened the door for me to discuss sexuality with her. It helped me get a handle on the experience of shame in my own life and how that was getting played out in my approach to my daughter's budding sexuality.

Petra: Yes, I gave it to my eldest daughter to read who is 15 years old. I hesitated at first because of the molestation incidents and because of the details of my first sexual experience. But I decided that the molestation story might help her awareness of the reality of sexual abuse and help think how she might set her own boundaries in the face of such a threat. I know that teens are sexually active younger now and, perhaps, knowing my story might encourage her to come to me when she considers having her first sexual experience.

Marley: Yes, I have told my daughter everything. I was as open and direct with her about my life as much as possible. I answered her questions about sexuality as very truthfully as I could from my heart. I made a conscious effort to teach her the difference between loving sex and empty sex, to guide her into understanding that there is a difference. My sexual history was difficult and not something to be especially proud of, and I wanted it to be better for her than it was for me.

There were four other participants who said they would be willing to share their story with their adolescent daughter(s). Two stated that they had shared some technical, non-personal information already with their daughters regarding menstruation, sexual intercourse, pregnancy, and prevention techniques for sexually transmitted diseases. The reasons they were willing to share their own stories now were: (a) "Now that my mother has died, I wish I could have known more personal things about her, so I don't want my daughter to have any regrets"; (b) "It would open up the communication between myself and my daughter"; (c) "There would be more trust between myself and my daughter"; (d) "I am no longer worried about my daughter knowing about my early sexual experiences"; and (e) "I believe I would seem more human (a real person) in her eyes if I shared."

PHASE TWO:
ADOLESCENTS' RESPONSES
TO MOTHERS' NARRATIVE ACCOUNTS

Participants

Our adolescent participants consisted of 12 Canadian females between the ages of 15 and 19. As previously mentioned, because we did not have consent from all the mothers to interview their own daughters, we recruited 12 adolescents who were not related or known to the mothers. One participant was Aboriginal, another was of Asian descent, and the remaining were Caucasian.

Data Collection

We presented 12 stories from the mothers to two focus groups of adolescent females. The participants each read one of the 12 stories so that everyone had a different story to respond to. The adolescents spent 60 to 90 minutes writing their responses followed by a two-hour, audiotaped discussion in the focus group. We were interested in exploring their responses to mothers' adolescent sexuality experiences. In their focus groups they wrote individual responses to each of four questions and then participated in a group discussion.

The questions were: (a) "After reading this story please write a response concerning what you think about this story, the feelings that this story evokes, or anything that comes to mind that you would like to share about this story?" (b) "How are your sexual experiences similar/different than this mother's account?" (c) "If this was your own mother's story, how would you respond to hearing it?" (d) "Would it be okay for your mother to tell you this story? Why or why not?" and (e) "Why do you think mothers do not share their adolescent sexuality stories with their adolescent daughters?"

Findings

The responses to the mother narratives pertain to "then versus now" distinctions. They believe that families now communicate about sex more openly and that there is more accessibility to birth control. They also believe that there has been a shift from shame about being sexually active to "celebrating your sexuality" and "doing it a lot younger." Three stated that they identified with many of the experiences that the mothers talked about and normalized the mother's sexual exploration.

However, the majority of the responses were critical of the mothers' parents' behaviour, claiming that the parents seemed to show little support for their daughters. For example, "Her parents set her up for the worst kind of experience by ignoring her sexual development." Another stated that in the story she read, she could not imagine being put in the situation of needing an abortion and not having parental support: "They would definitely be disappointed but they would never leave me alone in the hospital." These adolescents felt that some of the mother's choices led to "inappropriate" behaviour. They felt that "dangerous exploration and sexual activity" demonstrated low self-esteem. One adolescent stated that the description of masturbating and playing sexual games with her own sister "was a bit odd." Most felt that "unhappy" or "unhealthy" adolescent experiences could have negative implications for future relationships.

Adolescents Who Share: Similarities and Differences

The adolescent females identified few similarities between their own sexual experiences and the mothers' experiences, and several differences were noted between these mothers' stories and their own sexual experiences.

Similarities to mother's story. Similarities to the mothers' narratives pertain to the early sexual exploration of touching and playing games like "love." Some of the feelings that adolescents experience were similar such as, "When she talks about kissing her friend for practice or her obsession with breasts, I could really relate." Other similarities were hiding their sexual experiences from their parents, particularly, dating boys that their parents did not approve of and losing their virginity at approximately the same age.

Differences between mothers' and adolescents' experiences. The adolescent females discussed many differences between their own experiences and the mothers' stories. We highlight here the most common responses provided by these young women.

The adolescents stated that the idea of sex being shameful has changed and that sexual experimentation and sexual intercourse start earlier than in the mothers' narratives. "This mother talks about sex as being shameful in her time where as now I think it is more of a celebratory event of the shift from teenager to young adult. It is rare for a girl to be a virgin at 19 years of age now." "Sexual intercourse starts earlier these days." Also, they expressed that they saw sex more "as a way to please the woman as opposed to an act just to please the man." Overall, they felt that there was more sexual freedom now than in the early 1960s and 1970s.

Another major difference between the two generations was the opinion that there is more open communication about sex at school, within families, and between peers. "Mothering is different now than before." They felt that girls can now talk more to their parents about sex. They stated that there is more open communication about birth control and more access to birth control than in the mothers' era. One adolescent stated that her mother is different from the mother's parents in the narrative that she read, explaining that this mother's parents could not talk about sex because they feared she would start having sex: "My mother is very different from hers. My mother would never talk about sex of any kind with any of her children. However, this isn't because she believes that her children shouldn't be partaking, but more because I think she is just too embarrassed or nervous or maybe just doesn't know how to approach the topic." We note here that many mothers also felt that they would be too embarrassed to discuss sex with their own daughters, even though most adolescents in this study felt that there was more open communication between themselves and their mothers.

Several adolescents expressed more comfort with their own bodies. This comfort allowed them to be more exploratory and not fear intimacy as expressed in several mothers' stories. They stated they would not have sex "just to get it over with." Several mothers had stated that they had sex just to get it over with, but all of the adolescents in this study stated that they did not support this explanation for having sex. One adolescent did not agree with one mother's approach to celebrating her own daughter's sexuality:

> When she says at the end of her story that her daughter's sexual experiences need to be celebrated, I do not agree. It is really hard for daughters at that age to talk about sexual experiences. I have never spoken to my parents about my experiences yet I still enjoy them all the same. I think the issue is to make the daughter feel like it is okay to engage in sexual experiences at the right age but only talk about the actual experience if the daughter opens it up first because it seems like the mother is being a little selfish in trying to celebrate it with her daughter.

The adolescents in this study suggest many differences between their own experiences and the mothers, but the adolescents also disagree among themselves about what these differences are.

Adolescent Responses to "If This Was Your Mother"

In the following section, we present more specific answers to the remaining questions that we asked the adolescents about their own experiences with their own mothers and their views about their own mother's sexuality.

If this was your own mother's story, how would you respond? There were five main reactions to this question: feeling horrified, feeling embarrassed or awkward, being surprised, and being interested in knowing more. Several adolescents expressed being embarrassed yet interested at the same time. Only one adolescent stated she would feel "happy to hear" the mother's story if it were her own mother.

> I would feel happy to hear this story because a lot of the things she went through I did as well. I would like to know that she was responsible in having sex and also that she would be able to appreciate and understand the insecurities that I was having between grades 6 to 12.

Would you or would you not want your own mother to share? In response to this question, four adolescents answered with a clear "no." Five, however, responded that it would be okay to have their mothers tell them this story. One adolescent was tentative: "Okay but not likely," and two others stated that it would be "okay but it would be embarrassing." Those who did not want to hear their own mother's adolescent sexual narratives stated that it would be upsetting and make them feel less confident.

> It is safe and comfortable knowing what I know about my mother and I wouldn't want my perspective of her to change so dramatically. The only positive thing that I think I would get out of hearing this story from my mom would be the realization that she is a very strong woman to be able to have gone through these awful things in adolescence and still turn out to be the wonderful mother that she is.

The group that said they would want to know their own mother's stories was between the ages of 17 and 19, even though some felt that it would be unlikely that their mother actually would share.

> Yes, because there are so many times in your life when you are too embarrassed or shy to even ask your friends so if someone like your mother told you about her experiences instead of hunting it down yourself, this would provide a greater sense of self esteem for adolescents to know that the way they are feeling is normal and it would also increase the mother/daughter relationship by building trust.

One adolescent female concluded this question by stating that, "Looking at today's world through the media where every possible feeling and experience is thrown at you constantly, it seems funny that we still can't talk about things with our mothers."

Why do you think that mothers are not willing to share? The adolescents in this study felt that mothers do not share because their daughters might get embarrassed or, in contrast, mothers are too embarrassed to share. In essence, they do not have the kind of relationship where they can share these stories. Mothers also feared that daughters would get the wrong message, such as daughters "not waiting as long for sex" because if it was alright for "mother to do it, it's alright for her!" Further, mothers feared they would lose their daughter's respect because they felt ashamed of their own stories; it would most likely "shatter" their daughter's perspective of them as mother. They also felt the information they might share with their daughters was not as relevant today. Finally, mothers were trying to protect their daughters because they believed that "not talking about it" means "it won't happen." Another stated that she thought that mothers develop "barriers and it prevents them from talking about it."

COMPARING MOTHERS' STORIES
AND ADOLESCENT RESPONSES

The findings in the first phase of this study are conflictual and para-doxical. When the "would-share" group of mothers is compared to the "would-not-share" group of mothers interesting elements emerged. Generally, the "would-share" group's adolescent sexual experiences are more evocative, violent, and tragic. These stories are about surviving abuse and humiliation–a survivor's tale. The "would-not-share" group in comparison narrated stories that are generally more naive and innocent–tales of budding sexuality and sexual exploration.

The mothers who chose to remain silent assumed their daughters would not want to know about their adolescent sexual experiences. They believed that mothers should be framed as the "good-mother" figure: a mother whose sexuality must be kept private to prevent "embarrassment," "shame," or "humiliation." If mother is a sexual being she will lose "respect" and "dignity" and act "inappropriately." Although many of these mothers expressed a yearning to know more about their own mother's private lives, they believed they must protect their daughters from this aspect of their own womanhood.

On the other hand, mothers who chose to tell understood sharing their adolescent sexual experiences as a teaching tool. They believed that there was much for daughters to learn through the act of sharing. They wanted to protect their daughters from an unsafe world and to provide guidance or necessary knowledge to ensure their daughter's success in navigating the sexual terrain as a woman. They wanted to teach their daughters not to blame themselves for wanting to express their sexuality, that there was no need for shame, that they had a right to define their own sexuality, that they had choices in defining their own sexual practices and, as young women, they could set boundaries that met their own needs. On this point, we noticed clear differences between the two groups of mothers. Those who chose to remain silent considered their role as mother of primary importance and their sexual identity secondary. However, those who chose to tell their daughters primarily valued the safety of the emerging sexual development of their daughter(s), willing to put their image as mother aside.

As we investigate the reasons mothers gave for remaining silent and the claims that daughters made about not wishing to hear their mother's sexuality narratives, several of their arguments overlap. Both stated that it would change a daughters' image of her mother in a negative way–it would change a mother's "good-mother" status or shatter the daughter's "good-mother" image. It would upset daughters to know the details of their mother's sexual experiences. It would be embarrassing or shaming or uncomfortable for both mothers and daughters to have to share/listen to tales of adolescent sexuality. Both mothers and daughters stated that sharing would make them feel vulnerable, insecure, and less confident in their own roles. Mothers expanded on their reasons for not sharing that included other significant elements: it is inappropriate, taboo, not good to cross a sexual boundary, burdens the daughter, is a private matter, creates fears about being judged or rejected, and daughters would not understand and daughters don't really want to know. Mothers and daughters stated that not sharing the details of one's sexual experiences allowed both mothers and daughters to maintain their own self-respect and dignity. Paradoxically, some participants from both groups stated that it would be interesting to know the private lives of their own mothers. And further, the adolescent females in this study, as they projected their lives into the future, could foresee sharing their own lives with their own daughters and wanted their future daughters to know about their own adolescent sexual development. This is consistent with Brock and Henning's (1993) findings that daughters in their 30s wished they knew more about their mother's personal and sexual lives.

As we examined the findings, we noticed a possible bridge for constructing conversations about sexuality. Mothers who were willing to share and daughters who were willing to know their mother's stories believed that sharing would provide more open, honest, and "real" communication between mothers and daughters. Daughters yearned to be validated by their mothers and taught from personal experiences rather than sex education, classes, or books. Daughters felt that communicating with their mothers about sexual experiences would normalize their own experiences and give them more confidence in terms of their own sexual development. Mothers also expressed a desire to teach their daughters about sexual boundaries and wished to empower their daughters in their sexual development by speaking openly and sharing lessons learned.

IMPLICATIONS FOR PRACTICE

The findings of this study evoke many considerations for clinicians and educators working with adolescent females. The first implication deals with the provision of education for mothers and daughters related to female life span development and issues of identity. Education needs to include a critical examination of topics such as beliefs and attitudes about women's sexual development and the deconstruction of cultural norms that perpetuate the dichotomies that exist for women as mothers. As clinicians, educators, and parents we need to dispel the myths and stereotypes regarding mothers as nonsexual beings. In other words, we recommend further discussion with adolescents regarding the myth of the nonsexual mother as "good mother" and the sexual mother as "bad mother."

Another area of focus for practice is education about the female body as portrayed in popular culture. There is an abundance of current research on adolescent body image and we suggest that this literature needs to be expanded to include women across the life span. The general trend is to devalue and to denigrate the aging female body and some attempts are being made to dispel this perception in the media. For example, recent movies such as *Calendar Girls* and *Something's Got to Give* depict mid-life mothers as openly expressing their sexuality in both family and public domains. As parents, educators, and clinicians working with youth, we need to broaden youth's perspectives to include older, aging female and male body types and broaden the discourse on sexuality across the lifespan as healthy, "normal," and vibrant. Topics such as ageism, sexism, and marginalization that are detrimental to human sexual development and identity are worthy of exploration in both educational curriculum and parental conversations for the healthy development of our youth.

Creating realistic curricula that includes decision-making models based in "real life" circumstances is warranted. We believe that the current curriculum in schools does not inform or prepare our youth for the hard decisions that they will have to face in the social world: How to create a dialogue with parents about sexual topics; not only how to say no, but how to decide when to say no; how to know when to say yes; how to know when and what kind of birth control is best; information about sexual pleasure and sexual agency, to name a few topics. Curriculum needs to be more than a delivery of facts, it needs to deconstruct practices that create gendered and often oppressive life scripts. The curriculum needs to be dialogical and contextual–a living curriculum that addresses the actual lived experiences of our youth and furthermore acknowledges the complex interplay between identity, rights to privacy, and parental responsibilities.

REFERENCES

Arvay, M. (2003). Doing reflexivity: A collaborative narrative approach. In L. Finlay and B. Gough (Eds.), *Reflexivity: A practical guide for researchers in health and social sciences* (pp. 163-175). London: Blackwell Press.

Brock, L. J., & Hennings, G. H. (1993). Sexuality education. *Family Relations, 93*(42), 61-66.

Daniluk, J. C. (1998). *Women's sexuality across the life span: Challenging myths, creating meanings.* New York: The Guilford Press.

DiIorio, C., Kelley, M., & Hockenberry-Eaton, M. (1999). Communication about sexual issues: Mothers, fathers, and friends. *Journal of Adolescent Health 24*(3), 181-189.

Flaake, K. (1994). A body of one's own: Sexual development and the female body in the mother-daughter relationship. In V. J. van Mens & K. Schreurs (Eds.), *Daughtering and mothering: Female subjectivity reanalyzed* (pp. 7-14). New York: Taylor & Francis/Routledge.

Friedman, A. (1998). Sexuality and motherhood: Mutually exclusive in perception of women. *Sex Roles, 38*(9), *781-800.*

Hales, D. (1999). *Just like a woman: How gender science is redefining what makes us female.* New York: Bantam.

Hutchinson, M. K., & Cooney, T. M. (1998). Patterns of parent-teen sexual risk communication: Implications for interventions. *Family Relations, 47,* 185-194.

Kitzinger, S. (1995). *Ourselves as mothers: The universal experience of motherhood.* New York: Addison-Wesley.

Martin, E. (1987). *The woman in the body: A cultural analysis of reproduction.* Boston: Beacon Press.

Northrup, C. (1998). *Women's bodies, women's wisdom.* New York: Bantam.

O'Sullivan, L., Jaramillo, B., Moreau, D., & Meyer-Bahlburg, H. (1999). Mother-daughter communication about sexuality in a clinical sample of Hispanic adolescent girls. *Hispanic Journal of Behavioral Sciences, 21*(4), 447-469.

O'Sullivan, L., Meyer-Bahlburg, H., & Watkins, B. (2001). Mother-daughter communication about sex among urban African American and Latino families. *Journal of Adolescent Research, 16*(3), 269-292.

Pipher, M. (1995). *Reviving Ophelia: Saving the selves of adolescent girls.* New York: Ballatine.

Raffaelli, M., & Green, S. (2003). Parent-adolescent communication about sex: Retrospective reports by Latino college students. *Journal of Marriage & Family, 65*(2), 474-481.

Rosenthal, D. A., & Feldman, S. (1999). The importance of importance: Adolescents' perceptions of parental communication about sexuality. *Journal of Adolescence 22*(6), 835-851.

Rosenthal, D. A., Feldman, S., & Edwards, D. (1998). Mum's the word: Mothers' perspectives on communication about sexuality with adolescents. *Journal of Adolescence, 21*(6), 727-743.

Rothman, B. K. (1989). *Recreating motherhood: Ideology and technology in patriarchal society.* New York: W. W. Norton.

Simanski, J. W. (1998). The birds and the bees: An analysis of advice given to parents through the popular press. *Adolescence, 33*, 37-45.

Taris, T. W., & Semin, G. R. (1997). Quality of mother-child interaction, differences in sexual attitudes, and intergenerational disagreement on sexuality. *Early Child Development and Care, 136*, 65-78.

Walters, S. D. (1992). *Lives together/worlds apart: Mothers and daughters in popular culture.* Berkeley, CA: University of California Press.

Wolf, N. (1997). *Promiscuities: The secret struggle for womanhood.* Toronto, ON: Random House of Canada.

Yowell, C. M. (1997). Risks of communication: Early adolescent girls' conversations with mothers and friends about sexuality. *Journal of Early Adolescence, 17*(2), 172-196.

"I'm Stuck as Far as Relationships Go": Dilemmas of Voice in Girls' Dating Relationships

Elizabeth Banister
Sonya Jakubec

SUMMARY. This is a study of how heterosexual girls construct the meaning of their health issues within their dating relationships. We found that a number of barriers contributed to girls' difficulty with articulating their needs and desires in their romantic relationships. Adolescent girls who participated in our study blamed themselves for their boyfriends' abuse and lack of commitment and experienced their ability to speak in their own interests as compromised. Many of the girls experienced what researchers term an "impossible choice" between compromising self to maintain a relationship or compromising the relationship to maintain self. The dating relationship was predominantly determined by patriarchal and dualistic thinking that undercut healthy decision making. Assisting girls within supportive environments to reflect upon

Elizabeth Banister, RN, PhD, is Professor, School of Nursing, Faculty of Human and Social Development, University of Victoria. Sonya Jakubec, RN, BScN, MN, is a doctoral student, School of Nursing, University of Calgary.

Address correspondence to: Dr. Elizabeth Banister, School of Nursing, University of Victoria, Box 1700, Victoria, BC, V8W 2Y2, Canada (E-mail: ebaniste@uvic.ca).

The study was made possible by the generous funding of the Social Sciences and Humanities Council (SSHRC) and Canadian Institutes of Health Research (CIHR).

[Haworth co-indexing entry note]: " 'I'm Stuck as Far as Relationships Go': Dilemmas of Voice in Girls' Dating Relationships." Banister, Elizabeth, and Sonya Jakubec. Co-published simultaneously in *Child & Youth Services* (The Haworth Press, Inc.) Vol. 26, No. 2, 2004, pp. 33-52; and: *Working Relationally with Girls: Complex Lives/Complex Identities* (ed: Marie L. Hoskins, and Sibylle Artz) The Haworth Press, Inc., 2004, pp. 33-52. Single or multiple copies of this article are available for a fee from The Haworth Document Delivery Service [1-800-HAWORTH, 9:00 a.m. - 5:00 p.m. (EST). E-mail address: docdelivery@haworthpress.com].

gendered power differentials in their relationships can facilitate their expression of authentic voice which in turn can enhance their own health behaviors. *[Article copies available for a fee from The Haworth Document Delivery Service: 1-800-HAWORTH. E-mail address: <docdelivery@haworthpress.com> Website: <http://www.HaworthPress.com> © 2004 by The Haworth Press, Inc. All rights reserved.]*

KEYWORDS. Adolescent girls' health, adolescent dating

INTRODUCTION

Societal devaluation of adolescent girls may disempower them psychologically, making it difficult for them to consolidate their values and develop a strong sense of self in relationships (Brown, 1999; Giroux, 1998). This devaluation is manifested within power structures of heterosexual dating relations that are governed by strong social hierarchies and patterns that maintain subordinate social roles for women generally and young women specifically (Counts, 1999; Heise, 1998; King & Ryan, 2004). As Miller and Stiver (1997) assert, the power relationships inherent in patriarchal systems have a major negative impact upon adolescent girls' capabilities to make decisions about their health-related behaviour. For example, a girl may choose to compromise her own health by dismissing abuse, engaging in unprotected sex, or taking drugs rather than risk the loss of a dating relationship (Silverman, Raj, Mucci, & Hathaway, 2001).

In her examination of cultural influences on adolescent girls' health issues (such as eating disorders), Hoskins (2002) uses the notion of "self-creation," arguing that development of self is influenced by dominant cultural features conveyed, for example, by the media. The self exists in relationship, and the construction of relationships based on domination is therefore inherently a social issue. Self, according to Hoskins (2002) and Bohan (2002), exists in conversational exchange and is comprised of "culturally available symbols, metaphors, images, and actions from a variety of contexts" (Hoskins, p. 239). It is within this exchange that girls' voice, agency, and identity capital, as described by Cote and Schwartz (2002), is constructed.

Support for the notion of a socially constructed and context-sensitive self is provided by Smolak and Munstertieger (2002) in their study on gender differences and voice pertaining to eating disorders and depression. In their research they found that young women seem able to express themselves more openly within the company of other women. This phenomenon of girls' open expression of self is addressed in the literature through the notion of "authentic voice," a term used by cultural self-in-relation theorists such as Gilligan (1982) and Tolman (2002). Authentic voice becomes apparent as girls address such potentially morally challenging tasks as making decisions related to abortion or to the experience or expression of sexual pleasure.

However, some young women are not "speaking up" for themselves. For example, in girls' heterosexual romantic relationships it appears that social reinforcement of passivity silences some adolescent girls or deprives them of a voice (Gilligan, 1990). Social conditions such as these that limit girls' authentic voice can curtail their sense of intrinsic worth and can thus have damaging effects on their development and health, creating greater emotional needs for nurturance, affirmation, validation, and security (Smolak & Munstertieger, 2002). The subordination of girls' authentic voices to dominant discourses and stereotypical roles could be a contributor to health compromises, particularly abuse in relationships for girls (King & Ryan, 2004).

Gilligan (1991) argues that the expression of authentic voice as a means of sharing power in relationships becomes a barometer of relationship, insomuch as shared power contributes to more mutuality and authenticity in relationships that can create space for self and relationship development and thus of health status for adolescent women. A girl's understanding of herself in the world is facilitated through authentic, mutual connections with others (Jordan, 1993, 1997). Compromises to open, assertive, and authentic communication in dating relationships can affect this developmental task (Jordan, 1991).

Challenges to girls' expression of authentic voice may take a number of forms. As Lemkau and Lanau (1986) explain, if a girl attempts to enhance her social status by subordinating her authentic voice to the wishes of others (individual or societal), she may paradoxically undermine her self-esteem and health status. The privileging of males over females in our society and subordinating the voice of young women in the development of gender roles in adolescence is found to compromise adolescent female's mental health (Barrett & White, 2002). Girls (and their dating partners) are influenced by media images of the "good" woman who is "selfless" (King & Ryan, 2004), attends to her image, giving her appearance and body to others as a commodity (Kilbourne, 1995; Massie, 2000) and rarely expresses anger or asserts her needs, except at times towards other women (Artz, 1998; Lemkau & Landau, 1986).

The potential for health compromises is intensified when, in the context of a sexual relationship, a young woman succumbs to patriarchal interests that act to silence her voice and desire and her ability to speak to her own needs (Tolman, 1999). "Sexual authenticity" or one's ability to express and experience genuine sexual desire and pleasure within an intimate relationship is central to a woman's psychological health (Miller, 1976). Further, "*not* feeling sexual desire may put girls in danger and 'at risk'" (Tolman, 2002, p. 21, emphasis in original). When they disconnect from their sexual feelings, girls make themselves more vulnerable to what others are feeling and to others' dictates about what they should be feeling (again, both individually and socially). This can render girls incapable of negotiating sexual practices such as contraception use and "safer" sex (Holland, Ramazanoglu, Scott, Sharpe, & Thomson, 1990; Tolman, 2002).

In romantic relationships, girls may not express their needs, in compliance with the social norms that place high value on girls having a boyfriend, if they believe that expression of needs might jeopardize the relationship (van Roosmalen, 2000). Even though girls identify the need for open communication in relationships, many fear expressing themselves because of the chance of losing the socially valued role of girlfriend. Girls tend to silence their thoughts and feelings for the sake of preserving the relationship (Brown & Gilligan, 1992). In this case, relationship stability may be bought with compromises to self-esteem and health. Other reported negative consequences of romantic involvement for girls include difficulties with job and academic performance (Neeman, Hubbard & Masten, as cited in Compian, Gowan & Hayward, 2004).

Theoretical Perspectives

We approached this study from relational, feminist, and constructivist perspectives on human development. The relational perspective holds that adolescent girls develop their identity through their relationships with others (Gilligan, 1990; Sullivan, 1996). The feminist perspective attempts to assess power differentials and oppression (gendered or otherwise) that occur in social relationships. According to constructivist philosophy the meaning of girls' dating relationships is socially constructed; dating relationships are shaped by and evolve through negotiation within the relationships themselves (Locher & Prugl, 2001). Adolescent boys and girls construct the meaning of their dating relationships according to a disparity of power, weighing heavily on the side of boys. Girls' ability to make healthy dating decisions is compromised by this social order. According to Scott (as cited in Locher & Prugl, 2001), "Gender is a constitutive element of social relationships based on perceived differences between the sexes, and gender is a primary way of signifying relationships of power" (p. 116).

Our emphasis, then, in our synthesis of relational, feminist, and constructivist frameworks was on the process of identification, on the ways in which identity formation is related to gendered power, and on the way in which gender is structurally pervasive. In our analysis we recognize, as Alcoff (1994) and Haslanger (2000) do, that while there is a significant impact of gender on the self, women can be supported to critically question this construction within their romantic relationships. Important to our findings are ways in which individuals may develop the personal agency to resist social/political structures that impose a narrowly defined gendered identity.

This study was developed to explore the ways adolescent girls understand their health issues within the context of dating relationships. We posed the following question: "What are adolescent girls' health concerns within their dating relationships?" The goal was to listen to a small group of middle adolescent (ages 15-16) girls involved in heterosexual romantic relationships. A number of themes were elicited from the group conversations, some of which are reported elsewhere (Banister, Jakubec, & Stein, 2003).

METHOD

Ethical approval for the study was obtained through the university's research ethics board. We were also required to obtain approval from the local school board in order to access girls through the three local high schools. Prior to each initial group conversation, participants were informed of the limits of confidentiality and anonymity and of the choice to withdraw from the study at any time without any consequence. The girls were also informed of the importance of maintaining confidentiality within the groups; each group developed rules pertaining to this issue (Banister, 2002).

We located 40 adolescent girls, ages 15-16, for the study through three local secondary schools (including one designated as an alternative school), a local youth health clinic, and a rural First Nations secondary school. Participants were recruited through notices placed at each site and through site contacts such as school counselors, teachers, and a clinic nurse. Criteria for inclusion included girls who had been in a dating relationship for one month or longer and who were agreeable to participate in the groups. We had little difficulty accessing participants for the study and ascertained from this that staff and girls at each site placed a high value on adolescent girls' dating related health concerns and desired to learn more about such concerns.

Data were obtained through group conversations. Field notes were kept to record observations at each site, including non-verbal communication among focus group members and details of the larger social situation (such as informal interaction between girls and boys during school lunch breaks and the availability of adolescent sexual health information in the clinic waiting room). Researchers also kept notes to record their reflections, interpretations, and reactions to participants' accounts and to the context within which the accounts took place (Tedlock, 2000).

We conducted four 1-hour focus group conversations with girls at each of the five sites from September through December, 2001. Each group was made up of about 8 girls and was facilitated by one of five female graduate student research assistants. Prompts used in the group conversations to generate discussion around the topic of inquiry included: "Please describe your experience of your dating relationships?" "How might [these experiences] relate to your health?" The group sessions were tape-recorded and transcribed for analysis. Each interview was transcribed by a professional transcriber.

Broad abstract themes were developed from a process of reviewing categories (derived inductively), clustering categories into those that are similar and those that are different, and identifying patterns (Le Compte, 2000; Spradley, 1979). The themes represented a synthesis of participants' responses within and across group interviews that collectively captured their health concerns within their dating relationships. The emerging analysis was discussed with group participants throughout the research process for verification (Lincoln & Guba, 1985). The principal investigator also attended at least one meeting with each group for a credibility check to verify the accuracy of the themes.

FINDINGS

We will provide a brief overview of two themes that were prevalent within the group conversations that pertain to girls' voice. The first theme, "Like, I just don't know what to do!" illustrates the ways in which patriarchal social structures contribute to girls' experience of psychological stress in their intimate relationships with boys. The second theme, "Build up strength and back out of those situations," illustrates the form of communication within the groups that our research method fostered, as the girls' shared narratives reveal power differentials operating within relational constructions of love and sexual intercourse. We also explore how personal agency can be facilitated as a social intervention in the feminist approaches we utilized. Pseudonyms are used throughout to protect anonymity.

"Like, I Just Don't Know What to Do!": Silencing Voice

In the following interview excerpt, Liana shares her confusion about her dating relationship and desire to avoid conflict:

> Liana: Like, people get confused in relationships and they're stuck and they're, like, "What am I supposed to do? Should I stay here and be with somebody that wants to be with me although I'm getting abused and emotionally and physically put down and then . . . or should I leave and not have anything or anybody?"

When a romantic relationship reaches the point of causing more harm than good, a girl may choose between mutually exclusive options of caring for herself or caring for the relationship. Katie expresses the confusion and anguish that accompany her experience of conflicted needs within her relationship:

> Like, sometimes when we argue I try to back away just so I can have my time and my space to think of what's going on and I don't want to be with him but I do want to be with him. I talk to my friends about this kind of stuff but I don't know what to do anymore. It's, like, I'm trapped or something. I don't know.

Katie is experiencing a dilemma that could be described as an "impossible choice" (Spencer, 2000) between compromising self so as to maintain relationship or compromising relationship so as to maintain self (Gilligan, 1990). This dilemma can be a very serious matter for adolescent girls who may be subjected to violence, on the one hand yet, on the other hand, must bear the social and personal consequences of abandoning their social, personal, and emotional commitment to their boyfriend. For the girls, the consequences of "losing the guy" often outweighed the consequences of losing their voice within the relationship no matter how unhealthy the relationship might be. In this section we consider the dynamics and intricacies of a choice to compromise personal needs to save the relationship and fulfill socially designated roles.

The young women interviewed in this study experienced psychological distress over the uncertainty of their dating relationships, particularly concerning the relationships' stability and strength. This distress is consistent with the negative consequences understood as the invisible structural violence within our communities that influences psychological and physical ill health (James, Jenks, & Prout, 1998). Within an environment of uncertainty, participants provided numerous accounts of ruminating and second guessing "what [their boyfriends were] thinking and feeling," placing their needs into the background. To increase certainty in the absence of male commitment, they often assumed inappropriately high levels of responsibility within the relationship. In the following interview excerpt, Stephanie describes the distress she experiences in a relationship in which she feels responsible for its emotional health:

> You take all the emotional baggage for it, like, for the relationship. Girls totally do! They're the ones that go home and cry and think everything over and over, and they make things that won't even be true, but they exaggerate and imagine these things. You just think and over, [you] think too many things and you drive yourself crazy, like, "Well, what could I have said?" or "What did I do?"

Within a relationship characterized by poor communication, the girl would likely spend time second-guessing her dating partner's intentions and act on the basis of such speculation. Joireman, Parrott, and Hammer (2002) describe a "self-absorption paradox" whereby such rumination contributes to experiences of distress, isolating individuals from connecting to others. The paradox is both social and psychological in nature. The girls' preoccupations diverted attention from reflecting on the structural nature of their experiences or systematic changes they could participate in. Furthermore, such unproductive thought processes could interfere with the positive developmental effects of self-reflection and expression, which fosters empathy and healthy self-perspective (Trapnell & Campbell, 1999).

The issue of sexual intercourse was particularly problematic for authentic expression of voice within dating relationships, and consequences of the "negotiation" process could compromise identity development, the health of the girls, and the strength of girls' voices in other social contexts. Some of the girls described times they preferred not to have sex but went along with it to "please the guy":

> Breanne: I feel like a piece of meat. I do think sex is pretty gross sometimes, but I like sex. But sometimes you're not in the mood and stuff but if you totally are, then if you do [initiate sex], you feel kind of bad actually after.

> Sheena: I don't feel dirty or anything . . . but you're just, like, "I really didn't want to do that." But you just get into it because you know they want it. And then when they're not in the mood and you are they're just like, "Fuck off!"

> Breanne: This is really hard to explain . . . but it [having sex] makes you more confused after. I mean they can just leave if you don't want it, just go out with their friends and totally ignore you.

Such ambiguous situations of refusing and initiating or desiring and disliking sex can understandably create distress and uncertainty for the girls.

Girls' difficulty with expressing their needs and desires can have serious health consequences, particularly in the realm of safe sex negotiations. An excerpt from a group conversation illustrates girls' difficulties with voicing their needs and desires when it came to having "safe sex:"

> Suzanne: Sometimes you're scared to speak up. It's just stupid to ask your boyfriend to talk about safe sex. It's hard to explain. It's hard, uncomfortable.

> Marlee: It's hard to talk to a guy about safe sex. It's, like, uncool . . . you just *don't* do that.

These particular examples are telling because such responses to being in sexual relations are unmistakably genuine in that they articulate personal conflicting feelings and needs that challenge norms of female nurturance and caregiving established by social convention (Tolman, 2002). Many girls avoided difficult and "uncomfortable" conversations about the topic of safe sex and engaged in sexual activities that compromised both identity and health, believing that these choices would safeguard their romantic relationship.

In suppressing or denying her "socially unacceptable" authentic response (in the case of not meeting the sexual desires of her dating partner) and placing her boyfriend's needs over her own to increase relationship stability, a girl's emerging adult identity may be compromised, reinforcing the patterns that invalidate her voice (Tolman, 1999). In holding back part of herself in the appeasement of social roles she may descend into confusion, distress, self-doubt, and self-denigration; and she may jeopardize her plans for her own future. In the following interview excerpt, Jocelyn speaks of a decision she faced in order to keep her boyfriend; the decision could potentially have had an untoward impact upon all aspects of her life:

> I thought that if I got pregnant that he would dig me . . . he, like, made me so want to have kids for him.

Although prominent in sexual negotiations, the dynamic of compromising voice to preserve relationship was also apparent in other aspects of girls' dating relationships. One participant described how her own wishes and thoughts continued to get pushed to the background as her former boyfriend attempted to renew the relationship she wanted nothing to do with yet could not articulate this wish clearly and firmly to her partner:

> Aimee: He's, like, my ex-boyfriend. We've just recently broke up but he tried to come back to me and I'm trying to push away. And he's making it a lot harder on me because he's just pulling me in.

Aimee's voice was subordinated to responses deemed socially appropriate or expected by the boyfriend. This was the case for many of the girls in our study. Few participants provided descriptions of asserting their own concerns, thoughts, or feelings within their romantic relationships. Lisa described the confusion she experienced when her boyfriend attempted to exert control over her by telling her he was convinced she was cheating on him and that he wanted her to "be more like this or that." Ultimately she claimed, "I'm not even myself anymore. I've lost my personality. I lost my uniqueness."

Wanda describes a pattern of shifting her identity in attempting to meet the expectations of the other and reflects on the consequences of this for her mental health:

> Like, I've totally changed. I've changed my style in music, I've changed my style in clothes, everything. And even though when I

catch myself doing it, I have to stop and kind of realize it because if I'm not with a guy that's going to accept me for who I am, then I shouldn't want to be with him anyway. But every guy I've been with, I've always changed. Like, I'm a different person with every guy I go out with.

When girls empathize with their boyfriends' emotional pain, they may compromise their own wellbeing (Jordan, Surrey, & Kaplan, 1982); their work toward developing mutuality in their relationships can be counter-productive. For girls in this study, boyfriends' reactions and expression of their own personal distress over relationship disconnection aroused girls' empathy, so that even when a girl decided she needed to leave the relationship, it was not easy for her when her boyfriend cried and begged her to stay. In the following interview excerpt, Anna expresses her anguish over this "push and pull" of the relationship:

It confuses me . . . and he doesn't give me enough space for myself. I want some time away from him but he was crying and it's hard for me to deal with that. It is! It's hard. I can't cope with seeing a guy cry. It's really sad. It makes me sad.

The impossible choice of asserting one's voice, developing a sense of self, and possibly losing the relationship and its social consequences is a common conundrum for young women in their dating relationships. More often than not, girls tend to avoid conflict in their relationships; this and their firm desire to maintain relationships has a great influence on their choices regarding most aspects of their relationships (Tolman, 1999).

The difficulty with leaving a relationship is addressed by van Roosemalen (2000), who discusses the social status afforded young women in their relationships and by Jordan, Surrey, and Kaplan's (1982) discussions of women's empathy in relationships. For the girls in this study, leaving a relationship was both socially and personally challenging; for some, the risks of abandonment or of seeing the other hurting as a result of a break-up were more painful than the risks of being in an unsatisfactory or even dangerous relationship. Melinda explains:

That's how it was when I was going out with this guy named Neil. And we were together for, like, six months. And I was frustrated with him . . . that guy that was abusive, right? And I just left him and he was, like, sitting there crying away and crying away and I just didn't know what to do. And I felt bad. So, I took him back because I didn't like seeing him like that.

In Western culture, girls are inundated with harmful media images that purport to show how they should appropriately appear and behave in their relationships with young men (van Roosmalen, 2000; Vaughan & Fouts, 2003).

The patriarchal context within which girls' relational processes occur is a central source of relational disconnection and major contributing factor to psychological distress (Miller & Stiver, 1997). Many of the participants had not critically reflected upon their playing out of social roles, the influence of the media on their identity, or about their complicity in the perpetuation of roles that render them vulnerable. Alongside the lack of reflection, the girls also had few opportunities to develop ways to authentically voice their own needs in opposition to such roles. Without opportunities to see the gendered and social nature of their relational patterns, girls tend to evaluate themselves in accordance with norms that perpetuate the subordination and silencing of women's voices and, ultimately, hinder girls' self-development (Miller & Stiver, 1997).

The distress experienced by adolescent girls who faced the choice between forming connections and being true to their own experience, their "authentic voice," was made profoundly evident by the interviews conducted in this research. Girls work hard to maintain their dating relationships and spend copious amounts of time pondering how to do so. It also became evident through the focus groups that although the development of authentic voicing of experience was frequently impeded within the social context of their dating relationships, it was often fostered within other relational environments. Girls stated that opportunities for authentic expression were provided by conversations with some health professionals, parents, and peers. As reported in a recent study, young people continue to seek adult mentors for supportive and authoritative sexuality and relationship counsel (Planned Parenthood Association of British Columbia, Report of the Advocacy Committee, 2003). In our discussion of the second theme, we explicate the paradoxes surrounding voice experienced by the participants in their dating relationships and we explore the conditions necessary for them to construct a path out of this dilemma.

"Build Up Strength and Back Out of Those Situations": Possibilities for Voice and Healthy Relationships

A young woman speaks of her difficulties in finding support for herself, in addressing the difficulties of her relationship:

And I think one of the hardest things for me was in relationships where I was being abused and feeling like I couldn't talk to anybody about it and they wouldn't understand. And the people would judge me and I wouldn't get the support that I needed. In other cases, I was surprised from where it [support] came from and so I think my wish at this point is that we [girls in the focus group] develop a kind of network. You know, that we start with us and let it spread.

Similarly, Marcie stated, "There's no point in trying to talk to people about it because nobody is going to understand or nobody wants to understand or they're just trying to overcome their own problems." The above quotations indicate these participants' need for a form of support that was unavailable within their romantic relationships.

This section addresses the possibility of girls forming relationships outside of their romantic situations in which authentic voice is honoured. For some, such supportive relationships were not easy to find. Girls often expressed their frustrations that they had been unable to develop a mentorship that was not fraught with traditional patriarchal views and power relations. Through the course of the research, many of the girls constructed an understanding of the features and functions of this alternative sort of relationship.

Our goal was to listen for expression of their authentic voices, to capture their dating experiences in the stories. To do this, we knew that we would have to create an environment in which they could feel safe to talk and not be judged. Our interviews created an environment that had characteristics similar to those identified by the participants as helpful. Participants reported that the group provided a number of beneficial features. They expressed appreciation for an opportunity to listen to the narratives of others in the group: "You hear everybody else's problems . . . you don't feel so alone." Many found that hearing of others' varied experiences helped shift their perspectives. Two participants speak to this:

Danielle: I like hearing other people's point of view, so I think it kind of sometimes changes your point of view as well, which is good sometimes, or it just kind of makes you think of what you think.

Lana: And sharing, hearing other people's stories, you know, like, "I don't want to be like that" or "I want to be more like that," and [you] find your own way through other people's experiences.

In other cases, the benefits came from the sharing of useful information. For example, many spoke about the value of learning about sexual negotiations: "It is important to learn about how to have safe sex. There's a lot you have to learn."

Group members' stories provided girls with opportunities to hear about the ways in which a person can stay connected with herself and express herself authentically in relationships. Teresa shared her wish to "use [experiences of others] as a lesson." She went on to speak of the importance of sharing knowledge among peers about their dating relationships so that one may learn to identify when a relationship is becoming unhealthy:

> Teresa: If you're learning about how to develop your personal growth and learning about, as a girl, what you need, [you're] learning not to be stepped all over.

Jenn poignantly spoke to some painful learning about relationships through witnessing her mother's unhealthy intimate relationships:

> And watching that [her mother's repeated abuse by boyfriends], like, that's what I learned. And I was always, like, "I don't want to be like my mom at all." So I found a guy and he doesn't physically abuse me, he emotionally abuses me. And, like, it's *so hard*. Like, I know that I should get away from him and I, I can't, because it's too hard.

Although Jenn has not taken the steps needed to extricate herself from an abusive relationship, she has become aware to some degree of her situation. Another participant spoke of taking action in such situations:

> You're in a relationship, you're like, "Oh my God, I'm going to end up in that situation [an abusive relationship] if I don't get out this relationship that I'm in!" Because, "He's starting to do that kind of stuff," or whatever, so then you have to, like, build up strength, and back out of that situation.

As these excerpts show, hearing about others' experience provided these girls with a powerful opportunity for learning about relationships. Exposure to either positive options or problematic situations helped some of the girls envision potential consequences of various dating related interactions.

The girls learned that alternatives to the "impossible choice" could exist; that they could find a way to remain healthy and safe in their dating relationships. They identified that this healthy alternative would take the form of a relationship in which the other person would value them for who they were and would not judge their experience or demand compliance to external and quite possibly compromising criteria. One participant was clear in her assertion that judgment coming from the "other" is not appropriate in a supportive relationship and that valued connections can take place through a network or community rather than from someone in a position of authority. The girls identified what they needed to establish relationships that had these qualities.

In particular, the young women interviewed identified the value of support of peers and mentorship of other (often older) women in dealing with their relationships. Mentoring relationships in which older women act as advocates, validate girls' experiences, or foster their confidence are important for girls' development and psychological growth (Brown & Gilligan, 1992). This has been demonstrated, for example, to reduce risky sexual behaviour among adolescent women (Taylor-Seehafer & Rew, 2000).

Adolescence is an opportune time for positive change in health behaviors due to adolescents' increased capacity to think about the consequences of their dating interactions (Grasley, Wolfe, & Wekerle, 1999). Many of the girls were also learning about the relational aspects of self from observing and reflecting on the behaviour of others (peers, parents, teachers, etc). This was challenging and conflicted when some of their role models, such as their mothers, were in disconnected relationships themselves and were unable to help the girls reflect upon the influences on their relationships of patriarchal culture on subordinating their authentic voices. Melissa's statements illustrate this challenge:

> I grew up with my mom and she's always had a boyfriend and there was never a time when she was single for a long time. She always had a boyfriend. And there were different guys all the time. So I thought, like, you know, "You should have a boyfriend, they should be number one."

Experiences such as Melissa's, although unpleasant, provided the girls with an opportunity to critically reflect upon, analyze, and evaluate their own relationships. Reflection upon problematic life events is a discursive activity, facilitated by a supportive, questioning, and meaning-making environment. Beyond exposing participants to others' perspectives of relationships, the focus group environment provided a venue for the girls to exercise authentic expression. Once trust was established in the group, the girls were comfortable offering accounts of their dating relationships and providing or receiving suggestions and reactions. Peer sharing helped break participants' isolation and facilitated individuals' shifts in perspectives and in their behaviours. The following excerpt from a final group meeting in which girls were asked about their experience in the groups illustrates this point:

> It's helped to . . . hear other people's point of views and then kind of reflecting back on what I thought and then just thinking about what they do about it. It's just kind of helped deal with problems that I've had and hearing them say "Oh, I've been in that situation before." And then you kind of think, "Well, I guess it wasn't a big deal, like, I thought maybe it could only happen to me."

The support of the group helped participants to set aside some of their excessive rumination and worrying and to take greater responsibility for their relationships:

> I kind of found out that you shouldn't stress on, I shouldn't be stressing on things. It's not a big deal; it's just not a big deal. It's what happens in life, like, nothing to really stress about and get in a fight with yourself about it and "Oh man! What am I thinking? I'm so stupid. Such stupid problems and everyone goes through it." I'm kind of finding out, like, I get so worked up about things that don't really matter.

In this way the group served a positive purpose for the participants by enabling them, with its supportive and safe environment, to break their isolation and honor their developmental need for authentic connection. Within that context, each girl had the opportunity to discover her own voice through experimentation with expressing her experience in authentic ways.

DISCUSSION

This study was designed to explore the ways in which girls' health issues are constructed within the context of their dating relationships. Theoretical work and previous empirical findings related to girls' patriarchically constructed role in intimate relationships suggest that gender socialization processes and power relations are a major source of health difficulties for women (Miller & Stiver, 1997; van Roosemalen, 2000). Such processes disempower girls from acting in their own best interests and can threaten their abilities to protect and promote their own safety and health. Our data revealed ways in which dating relationship dynamics can compromise girls' development and health. The participants in our study experienced conflict as they struggled with the developmental task of formulating an identity characterized by assertiveness, self-confidence, and the ability to form intimate relationships based in authentic feelings.

It is important for helping professionals to develop a broad and holistic understanding of the dialectical struggle that occurs in the lives of adolescent women between a sense of self that assumes male domination and may compromise women's health and the identity that women construct dialogically in mutual caring relationships that empowers them to behave in health-promoting ways (Holland, Ramazanoglu, Scott, Sharpe & Thomson, 1990). It is important that we develop broad and holistic understandings of the power dynamics operating within adolescent romantic heterosexual relationships and constructions of gender identities which underlie them.

For the most part, adolescent girls are unaware of power differentials and inequities inherent in Western society's constructions of romantic relationship (Holland, Ramazanoglu, Scott, Sharpe & Thomson, 1990). This study addresses the need for health-related research to focus on gender violence and coercion and the need for developing an in-depth understanding of these aspects of dating relationship experiences.

REFERENCES

Alcoff, L. (1994). Cultural feminism versus post-structuralism: The identity crisis in feminist theory. In N. B. Dirks, G. Eley, & S. B. Ortner (Eds.), *Culture/power/history: A reader in contemporary social theory*. Princeton: Princeton University Press.

Artz, S. (1998). Where have all the school girls gone?: Violent girls in the school yard. *CYC Forum, 27*(2), 77-109.

Banister, E. (2002). Considerations for research ethics boards in evaluating qualitative studies: Lessons from the field with adolescent females. *Annals of the Royal College of Physicians and Surgeons of Canada, 35*(8), supplement, 567-570.

Banister, E., Jakubec, S., & Stein, J. (2003). "Like, what am I supposed to do?": Power, politics, and public health concerns in adolescent women's dating relationships. *Canadian Journal of Nursing Research, 35*(2), 16-33.

Barrett, A. E., & White, H. R. (2002). Trajectories of gender role orientation in adolescence and early adulthood: A prospective study of the mental health effects of masculinity and femininity. *Journal of Health and Social Behavior, 43*, 451-468.

Bohan, J. S. (2002). Sex differences and/in the self: Classic themes, feminist variations, postmodern challenges. *Psychology of Women Quarterly, 26*, 74-88.

Brown, L. M., & Gilligan, C. (1992). *Meeting at the crossroads: Women's psychology and girls' development.* New York: Ballantine Books.

Compian, L., Gowan, L. K., & Hayward, C. (2004). Peripubertal girls' romantic and platonic involvement with boys: Associations with body image and depression symptoms. *Journal of Research on Adolescence, 14*(1), 23-47.

Cote, J. E., & Schwartz, S. J. (2002). Comparing psychological and sociological approaches to identity: Identity status, identity capital, and the individuation process. *Journal of Adolescence, 25*, 571-586.

Counts, D., Brown, J., & Campbell, J. C. (1999). *To have and to hit: Cultural perspectives on wife beating.* Chicago: University of Illinois Press.

Gilligan, C. (1982). *In a different voice.* Cambridge, MA: Harvard University Press.

Gilligan, C. (1990). Joining the resistance: Capital psychology, politics, girls and women. *Michigan Quarterly Review, 29*(4), 501-531.

Gilligan, C. (1991). Women's psychological development: Implications for psychotherapy. *Women & Therapy, 11*, 5-32.

Giroux, H. A. (1998). Teenage sexuality, body politics, and the pedagogy of display. In J. S. Epstein (Ed.), *Youth culture: Identity in a postmodern world* (pp. 24-55). Malden, MA: Blackwell.

Grasley, C., Wolfe, D. A., & Wekerle, C. (1999). Empowering youth to end relationship violence. *Children's Services: Social Policy, Research, and Practice, 2*(4), 209-223.

Haslanger, S. (2000). Gender and race: (What) are they? (What) do we want them to be? *Nous, 34*(1), 31-55.

Heise, L. (1998). Violence against women: An integrated, ecological framework. *Violence Against Women, 4*, 262-290.

Holland, J., Ramazanoglu, C., Scott, S., Sharpe, S., & Thomson, R. (1990). Sex, gender and power: Young women's sexuality in the shadow of AIDS. *Sociology of Health and Illness, 12*(3), 336-350.

Hoskins, M. L. (2002). Girls' identity dilemmas: Spaces defined by definitions of worth. *Health Care for Women International, 23*, 231-247.

James, A., Jenks, C., & Prout, A. (1998). *Theorizing childhood.* Cambridge: Polity Press.

Joireman, J. A., Parrott, L., & Hammer, J. (2002). Empathy and the self-absorption paradox: Support for the distinction between self-rumination and self-reflection. *Self and Identity, 1*, 53-65.

Jordan, J. V. (1991). The movement of mutuality and power. *Work in progress # 53.* Wellesley, MA: Stone Center Working Paper Series.

Jordan, J. (1993). The relational self: A model of women's development. In J. van Mens-Verhulst, K. Schreurs, & L. Woertman (Eds.), *Daughtering and mothering: Female subjectivity reanalyzed* (pp. 135-144). New York: Routledge.

Jordan, J., Surrey, J., & Kaplan, A. (1982). Women and empathy. *Work in progress #2.* Wellesley, MA: Stone Center Working Paper Series.

Kilbourne, J. (Director/Producer) (1995). *Slim hope: Advertising and the obsession with thinness.* [Motion Picture]. (Available from Media Education Foundation, 60 Masonic Street, Northampton, MA 01060).

King, M. C., & Ryan, J. M. (2004). Nursing care and adolescent dating violence. In J. Humphries & J. C. Campbell (Eds.), *Family violence and nursing practice* (pp. 288-306). Philadelphia: Lippincott, Williams & Wilkins.

LeCompte, M. D. (2000). Analyzing qualitative data. *Theory into Practice, 39*(3), 146-154.

Lemkau, J. P., & Landau, C. (1986). The "selfless syndrome": Assessment and treatment considerations. *Psychotherapy: Theory, research, and practice, 23,* 227-233.

Lincoln, Y. S., & Guba, E. G. (1985). *Naturalistic inquiry.* Beverley Hills, CA: Sage.

Locher, B., & Prugl, E. (2001). Feminism and constructivism: Worlds apart or sharing the middle ground. *International Studies Quarterly, 45,* 111-129.

Massie, E. (Director/Producer) (2000). *What a girl wants.* [Motion Picture]. (Available from Media Education Foundation, 60 Masonic Street, Northampton, MA 01060).

Miller, J. B., & Stiver, I. P. (1997). *The healing connection.* Boston: Beacon Press.

Miller, J. B., & Stiver, I. P. (1991). A relational reframing of therapy. *Work in Progress, No. 52.* Wellesley, MA: Stone Center Working Paper Series.

Planned Parenthood Association of British Columbia (PPABC) (2003). *The right to health education in schools: A stakeholder analysis.* Planned Parenthood Association of British Columbia, Report of the Advocacy Committee. Vancouver, BC, Canada.

Silverman, J. G., Raj, A., Mucci, L. A., & Hathaway, J. E. (2001). Dating violence against adolescent girls and associated substance use, unhealthy weight control, sexual risk behaviour, pregnancy and suicidality. *The Journal of the American Medical Association, 286*(5), 572-579.

Smolak, L., & Munstertierger, B. F. (2002). The relationship of gender and voice to depression and eating disorders. *Psychology of Women Quarterly, 26,* 234-241.

Spradley, J. P. (1979). *The ethnographic interview.* New York: Holt, Rinehart & Winston.

Spencer, R. (2000). A comparison of relational psychologies. *Project report, No. 5.* Wellesley, MA: Stone Center Working Paper Series.

Sullivan, A. M. (1996). From mentor to muse: Recasting the role of women in relationship with urban adolescent girls. In B. J. Leadbeater & N. Way (Eds.), *Urban girls: Resisting stereotypes, creating identities* (pp. 226-253). New York: New York University Press.

Taylor, J. M., Gilligan, C., & Sullivan, A. (1995). *Between voice and silence: Women and girls, race and relationship.* Cambridge, MA: Harvard University Press.

Taylor-Seehafer, M., & Rew, L. (2000). Risky sexual behavior among adolescent women. *Journal of the Society of Pediatric Nurses, 5*(1), 15-25.

Tedlock, B. (2000). Ethnography and ethnographic representation. In N. K. Denzin & Y. S. Lincoln (Eds.), *Handbook of qualitative research* (2nd ed.) (pp. 455-486). Thousand Oaks: Sage.

Tolman, D. L. (1999). Dimensions of desire: Bridging qualitative and quantitative methods in a study of female adolescent sexuality. *Psychology of Women Quarterly, 23*(1), 7-39.

Tolman, D. L. (2002). *Dilemmas of desire: Teenage girls talk about sexuality.* Cambridge, MA: Harvard University Press.

Trapnell, P. D., & Campbell, J. D. (1999). Private self-consciousness and the five factor model of personality: Distinguishing rumination from reflection. *Journal of Personality and Social Psychology, 76*, 284-304.

van Roosemalen, E. (2000). Forces of patriarchy: Adolescent experiences of sexuality and conceptions of relationships. *Youth and Society, 32*(2), 202-227.

Vaughan, K. T., & Fouts, G. T. (2003). Changes in television and magazine exposure and eating disorder symptomatology. *Sex Roles, 49*(7/8), 313-321.

A Mediated Lifespace:
Working Relationally with Girls

Marie L. Hoskins
Lindsay C. Mathieson

SUMMARY. A lifespace has to do with how selves are mediated by combining multiple cultural symbols to construct an identity in the world. The authors cite examples from media texts, as well as from a narrative study conducted with 10 adolescent girls in a treatment program for eating disorders, that illustrate the importance of practitioners considering the lifespace when working with adolescent girls. A fuller understanding is needed of how societal influences such as media, globalization, gender, and body image impact girls' lives in significant ways. Although there are no set formulas for working with this kind of knowledge, there are strategies that can be used to raise one's awareness as a practitioner working with girls. Such strategies include challenging one's assumptions about gender stereotypes, refining and elaborating

Marie L. Hoskins, PhD, is Associate Professor, School of Child and Youth Care, Faculty of Human and Social Development, University of Victoria. Lindsay C. Mathieson, BSc, is a research assistant, School of Child and Youth Care and Department of Psychology, University of Victoria.

Address correspondence to: Dr. Marie L. Hoskins, School of Child and Youth Care, Faculty of Human and Social Development, University of Victoria, Box 1700, Victoria, BC, V8W 2Y2, Canada (E-mail: mhoskins@uvic.ca).

The study was made possible by the generous funding of the Social Sciences and Humanities Council (SSHRC).

[Haworth co-indexing entry note]: "A Mediated Lifespace: Working Relationally with Girls." Hoskins, Marie L., and Lindsay C. Mathieson. Co-published simultaneously in *Child & Youth Services* (The Haworth Press, Inc.) Vol. 26, No. 2, 2004, pp. 53-74; and: *Working Relationally with Girls: Complex Lives/Complex Identities* (ed: Marie L. Hoskins, and Sibylle Artz) The Haworth Press, Inc., 2004, pp. 53-74. Single or multiple copies of this article are available for a fee from The Haworth Document Delivery Service [1-800-HAWORTH, 9:00 a.m. - 5:00 p.m. (EST). E-mail address: docdelivery@haworthpress.com].

meaning-making questions, and resisting the restrictive discourses that inhibit girls' development. *[Article copies available for a fee from The Haworth Document Delivery Service: 1-800-HAWORTH. E-mail address: <docdelivery@haworthpress.com> Website: <http://www.HaworthPress.com>*

KEYWORDS. Constructivism, lifespace, identity, adolescent girls, eating disorders, media, feminism, youthwork, youth work

While reading a British newspaper, the *Daily Mail*,[1] during a recent trans-Atlantic flight, I (Hoskins) began to notice how women's lives were portrayed. One article, entitled "A Glass of Their Own: Hard Drinking British Women Are the Booziest in Europe," on the drinking habits of young women aged 18 to 24 years old reported that British women drink four times more than Italian women and substantially more than women from other European countries. Researcher Andrew Russell blames this increase in drinking on the trend towards growing independence among young women. "A whole generation of teenagers have been told they can do whatever the boys do–and that applies to drinking too" (p. 27). A few pages later I encountered another report about a 17-year-old girl who agreed to have sex with a soccer player and was attacked by up to seven others ("Police Quiz Top Players"). A party organizer claimed that girls are regularly "shared out" for sex among soccer stars–a practice known as "roasting" (p. 31). Another reporter covered a story that highlighted the impact on a teenager's self-esteem after having sex on a reality TV show (Conlan & Yaqoob, 2003). Afterwards, this young girl cried: "I feel dirty in myself and ashamed of what I've done. I do it because I feel that some of them [boys] want me" (p. 5).

These disturbing articles were sprinkled throughout the paper which also reported trivial news items such as female stars having bad hair days, one poor rock star who was losing her hair because of all the experimental colors she had tried over the years, and another list of women who appeared to be going down the same dangerous road. A full-page coverage of a fashion event attended by Camilla Parker Bowles (who confessed she really needed to get a pair of jazzy tights to spice up her image) was also included. Later in the paper there were two full pages devoted to what other guests of the event had chosen (rightly, but mostly wrongly) to wear.

I continued reading, hoping to find an article that portrayed women, or even one woman, in a positive light. At last I found an article describing the long time BBC arts correspondent, Joan Bakewell. Her career highlights, including several distinguished awards for journalism, were reassuring given that few women had been able to break into such a male dominated field. I read on, intrigued by how Ms. Bakewell had managed to hold her ground and carve a life for herself despite the multitude of hurdles she encountered. So far, so good, I thought to myself, until I read the next line: "Joan Bakewell was dubbed as the thinking man's crumpet because of her combination of looks and intelligence" (p. 56). "What kind of nonsense is this?" I wondered. "Oh, I see, it was said by a well-respected male colleague who decided to give her this cute label in 1988." And here it was, more than a decade later, still being quoted. Even in the title (which I had neglected to read earlier), "The TV Crumpet Who Was the Toast of Her Time," she has been rendered as an object to be consumed, albeit by thinking male consumers.

Perhaps most alarming for me was what I encountered in the two-page centrefold. In bold, large print was the title, "The Boys Who Could Beat the World." Admittedly, I was relieved as I continued reading when I realized the reporters were really just referring to an upcoming international rugby match, not an entire overthrow of the United Nations or even anything close to that kind of feat. But there was still something very troublesome about how these boys were described. Touted as British heroes with no mention of their fashion decisions, the reporter went on to say that we, as readers, were privy to a "fascinating glimpse of heroes in the making" (p. 48).

There is nothing remarkable about the way in which I noticed these gendered portrayals in the media. I simply selected a newspaper while boarding an airplane. I did not specifically seek out sexist magazines so that I could critique blatantly obvious images of women as objects.

Instead, I did what several others were doing in a public space: I read articles and observed images in a widely circulated British newspaper. And while reading, it was impossible to not notice such obvious contrasts in the ways in which men and women were represented. Men were commonly portrayed as heroes because of their athletic prowess, and women were portrayed as either successful or unsuccessful because of their appearance. These contrasts between genders are not new; women have throughout the centuries been prized for their beauty and passivity. What *is* new, however, is the easy access that we all have to these texts and images in the various locations of our lives.

For example, Grodin and Lindlof (1996) point out that "the place-ment of televisions in public spaces such as restaurants, malls, and air-ports changes the nature of social interaction and, consequently, the way individuals experience themselves in relation to others" (p. 3). Even if individuals choose to turn away from television in their own homes, it is now impossible to escape the constant infiltration of medi-ated environments in everyday life, yet the profound impact of mass communication on the human psyche has yet to be fully acknowledged in human service research and practice.

In the midst of these glaring media contrasts between men and women that can be found in such ordinary places as daily newspapers, airports, and restaurants, certain segments of our society are struggling with issues of identity. Such struggles manifest themselves in different ways such as aggression, gang membership, confusion and distress over sexual orientation, excessive drug and alcohol use, and disordered eat-ing. It is this last manifestation, disordered eating, that we have chosen to use as a background for this chapter.

In no other context is the issue of female identity so complex and challenging as it is in the development of disordered eating. Girls, not boys, are the main carriers and sustainers of the phenomena of anorexia nervosa, bulimia nervosa, and other categories of disordered eating. Given this gendered epidemiological profile, one might assume that an entry point into our understandings of these phenomena would begin with discussions of how gender works in our society. Yet in conversa-tions with girls who are engaged with us in a current research project and in conversations with practitioners, we observed little mention of how gender relations are enacted and embodied in everyday life.

THE LIGIA PROJECT

In this study, funded by the Social Sciences and Humanities Re-search Council of Canada and called the LIGIA Project (Listening to In-terpretations of Girls' Identities of Adolescence), we are attempting to understand how girls make sense of discourse (symbols, metaphors, im-ages, scripts, rules, norms, and narratives) in order to organize or con-struct their lives. We take the position that an eating disorder is the site where issues of identity, gender, and culture are made visible, particu-larly when girls have opportunities to articulate their interpretations. Through dialogues with participants, we enhanced our understanding of not only the processes of stability (what sustains the phenomenon) and change (what alleviates the phenomenon) but also how cultural practices are interpreted and integrated into girls' constructions of self, body, and world. Our three primary objectives for the study were the following:

1. To explicate adolescent girls' interpretations of cultural expectations and their evolving sense of themselves.
2. To apply a narrative analysis in order to increase understanding of how girls' identities are created, how identities are enabled, and how healthy identity development can be fostered.
3. To increase knowledge and understanding of the intersections and interrelationships between the development of identities and the cultural context in which adolescent girls live.

The research was guided by a number of framing questions including the following: What does listening to girls reveal about our culture and the process of taking up gendered identities? How do girls embody "acts of meaning," derived from cultural ecologies? What kinds of exclusions, injustices, inequities, and shortages of care in the existing world does this knowledge uncover? What kind of future for adolescent girls do these new understandings suggest?

We interviewed 10 adolescent girls, aged 13 to 18, who were in an eating disorders treatment program located in a hospital. Each girl was interviewed three times, with interviews lasting approximately 1 hour each. There was a 1 to 2 week time gap between interviews. Topics addressed in the interviews included media and popular culture (including television, magazines, music, movies, advertising, shopping, consumerism), how someone changes, happiness (what constitutes an ideal life), competition, peer relations, the experience of having an eating disorder, others' perceptions of girls with eating disorders, school experiences, drug use, family relations, and societies' rules for girls.

Following the participants' lead, probes were used to (a) elicit subjective meanings of their experiences, (b) illuminate significant events and processes that foster or inhibit their ability to be themselves, and (c) explicate the intersections and relationships between their identity development and the social context and culture in which they live.

Each interview was transcribed verbatim. This included highlighting the language, metaphors, and symbols the participants used to communicate an evolving understanding of their identity. Subsequently, the discourses (language, practices, symbols, and systems of knowledge) that surrounded their descriptions of various experiences were analyzed.

In essence, what we hoped to understand more fully was the depth and breadth of the lifespace of the girls we interviewed and how such spaces were located within larger cultural domains. Although the term lifespace is widely used in various human service professions, in our review of the literature we encountered vague and contradictory meanings. Further, we found articles describing the term as valuable as a practice intervention, but few focused on the value of understanding lifespace in research.

UNDERSTANDING THE LIFESPACE

Most professionals in the field agree that it is essential that we adopt holistic, contextually based approaches when working with families experiencing difficulties. All individuals construct lives for themselves from what is available in their environment (see for example, Harre & Gillett, 1994; Mahoney, 1991). Redl (1982) argued that practitioners should take into account situation and context when working with children and youth. Furthermore, the needs of different children need to be addressed and a variety of programs need to be implemented to meet these differences. In addition, he stated that "We as child care workers must become experts in creating life spaces for children" (p. 9). According to Gibson (2000), "What Redl meant by the term *life space* was that area of shared life experience between child and adult and frequently other children" (p. 39, emphasis in original).

Krueger and Stuart (1999) also emphasize the importance for child and youth care workers to be competent in specific contexts: "The challenge for the worker is to develop the knowledge, skill, and analytic ability to recognize, change, and/or create context" (p. 197). They discuss three aspects of context, namely, the meaning (ascribed by both the worker and youth), atmosphere, and nature of the interaction or activity. However, context in this case is limited to a very specific interaction or activity. Although they do not use the term lifespace, their discussion of context is similar to what Redl named lifespace. While this more narrowly defined context is important to consider in working with children and youth, we must also consider a macro-contextual space, or the lifespace more broadly defined, of the children and youth with whom we relate to in practice and research.

As previously mentioned, after consulting a number of journals from across a variety of disciplines within human development and social sciences, we conclude that lifespace is not consistently defined within a discipline or across disciplines. It is a term loosely defined and can be used to talk about specific contexts, particular techniques used in working with children and youth, or a more sophisticated interaction between the individual and environment.

For example, lifespace is a term often used in conjunction with Life Space Interviewing. This technique, developed by Redl and used by workers who are in direct contact with the child/youth, ". . . involves the child in a thinking and planning process aimed at increasing social, emotional and behavioral competence" (Gibson, 2000, p. 40). Similarly, another technique that incorporates the concept of lifespace is the Family Life Space Diagram (Motswin, 1980, cited in Barker, Barker, Dawson, & Knisely, 1997). The Family Life Space Diagram has been used in studies of sexual abuse survivors and their relations to abusers, family members, and significant others. This method includes using ". . . symbols to represent living entities within a defined life space" (p. 438). Therefore, the lifespace consists of the individual in relation to other individuals.

A special issue of the *Journal of Youth and Adolescence* was devoted to "the changing life space of early adolescence." In one article of this issue (Larson & Richards, 1989), lifespace was defined as the context in which adolescents develop. The focus was on daily activities: "What they [adolescents] do, who they do it with, and where they do it" (p. 502). Activities that were examined included "school work, maintenance, talk, media use, sports" (Richards & Larson, 1989, p. 617). The authors also looked at adolescents' subjective perceptions of their participation in these activities.

Lifespace has also been defined as "physical, mental, social, and spiritual aspects" of an individual (Hedelin, 2001, p. 401), while others talk about lifespace as an ecological context, including multiple life roles, environment and family, perceptions of a person and of others in his/her life, and that person's interactions with others (Szymanski, 1994). In the latter article, the author chose to focus on three elements of lifespace, family, culture, and community, in discussing life transitions of children with special needs or who are in rehabilitation.

These definitions and usages of the term lifespace raise many questions that need to be addressed. For example, who constructs a lifespace? As previously noted, Redl (1982) and Krueger and Stuart (1999) discuss the importance of child and youth care workers in creating lifespaces and contexts, respectively. Some researchers talk about individuals actively constructing a lifespace. For example, Oyserman and Swim (2001) suggest that individuals belonging to minority groups who have been stereotyped or discriminated against ". . . actively attempt to construct a buffering life space" (p. 1). Because of the inconsistency in definitions in the literature, it is important to have a clear definition of what a lifespace is in order to talk about it in depth and to apply it to practice and research situations.

Lewin (1954) originated the use of the term. Lewin described the lifespace as composed of the person and the environment, and he talked about these as being "*one* constellation of interdependent factors" (p. 919, emphasis in original). That is, the environment is dependent on the person and vice versa. Furthermore, he stressed the importance of viewing the lifespace as a whole (Lewin, 1936).

Lewin (1954) also acknowledged that the environment included both physical and social aspects, and that "It is important . . . to know the physical and social conditions because they limit the variety of possible life spaces" (p. 920). Lewin also pointed out that we cannot underestimate the importance of the social context; it is "at least as important as the physical" (p. 920). These points are particularly relevant when working with girls, recognizing the social and physical conditions that limit their options, including their options of how to behave, who to be, and what resources are available to them.

Lewin (1954) explained the psychological aspect of the lifespace, using three concepts: force, position, and potency. First, the force is a person's drive. This is described as a person's "tendency to act in a certain direction" (p. 923). Second, the position of an individual in relation to other parts of the lifespace is extremely important. Position determines the quality of a person's environment and his/her possibilities for the future. Third, potency refers to the importance of various aspects of the lifespace. That is, different elements of a person's lifespace are relatively more or less important.

Lewin further described in depth the boundaries and limitations of lifespaces and how this influences children: "The relation between accessible and inaccessible regions in the life space, the size of the space of free movement, and the precision of boundary between accessible and inaccessible areas are of great importance for behavior and development of the normal and abnormal child" (p. 925).

Similarly to how Krueger and Stuart (1999) discuss the meaning of a given context, Lewin (1936) noted that individuals will ascribe different meanings to different situations. He notes that the ". . . situation must be represented in the way in which it is 'real' for the individual in question" (p. 25). He also points out that even within the same individual, an identical environment can be given different meanings under different circumstances.

Finally, what arises out of Lewin's discussion of the lifespace is the idea that what should be of interest is processes instead of objects and changes of states instead of simply states themselves.

We agree with many of the aspects of what Lewin says about lifespaces. We think that it is important to recognize the conditions and boundaries of lifespace. We also believe that individuals are actively engaged in constructing meanings from and within their surroundings and, therefore, an individual's lifespace is constantly shifting and evolving. Lewin's theorizing on lifespaces occurred prior to the propagation of media and the widespread use of technology such as the Internet. One could argue that the media could be incorporated into Lewin's definition of lifespace by categorizing it as a social aspect of the lifespace. However, due to the fact that media has become so pervasive in our lives and that so many elements of media are geared towards adolescents with a specific purpose (i.e., to create a desire or need in them to purchase a product), the concept of lifespace needs to be modernized to include media. That is, we need to emphasize how selves are mediated by combining multiple cultural symbols to construct an identity in the world and, furthermore, acknowledge that such mediating processes work dialectically with media and other cultural influences.

We also believe that lifespaces are not neutral; they are imbued with power relations. If we consider the many ways that people create meaningful lives despite discriminating structures, then we believe it is timely as a group of professionals to extend our thinking on what it means to work with the lifespace of girls.

WORKING WITH THE LIFESPACE OF GIRLS

One way to begin to expand our understanding of girls' lifespace is to try to understand the influences that shape processes of identity for adolescent girls. Often practitioners work from early developmental theories (e.g., psychoanalytic theory) that were conceptualized prior to the proliferation of mediated environments (e.g., television, internet, music video, and other technological communications). Such developmental theories conceptualized the self as unitary, singular, and bounded. But newer, postmodern theories of self and identity caution practitioners from taking such traditional views of selfhood. Selves, from a postmodern perspective, acknowledge the multiple, evolving, transitory, relational nature of self-making that is indicative of the complexities of contemporary societies (Gergen, 1991, 1996; Mahoney, 1991).

Given the emphasis on self-in-relation that these contemporary models suggest, a fundamental revision needs to occur. For the most part this means taking an interest in cultural artifacts (symbols, images, metaphors, traditions, sites of resistance) and other aspects of popular culture that girls relate to when constructing their identities. Working with the lifespace involves much more than exploring family life, school environment, peer relationships, and so on. What is needed is a basic understanding of how identities are created in an information age and a consumer culture.

This is important because disordered eating is a prevalent mental health concern in North America for adolescent girls. If we acknowledge that we are awash in consumer culture in North America (see Bordo, 1993; Brumberg, 1997; Faludi, 1991), it is pertinent to inquire into how adolescent girls negotiate their way through a complex maze of signs and signifiers. There are several aspects related to the processes of integrating various cultural artifacts into self-identities that need to be considered.

For example, Bordo (1993) suggests that the influence of media on people's experience or lifespace can be likened to a conversation. Some parts of the conversation resonate with their experience, and others evaporate when they are not meaningful enough to be remembered. Memory and meaning function are integrated in often chaotic and non-linear ways. Both speaker and listener contribute to the conversational space or what some refer to as the "dialogical space" (Gergen, 1996). Facts, ideas, emotions, stories, values, and so on are all exchanged in dialogue with others. As communicators who have the capacity to speak (to voice) and take in information, we can converse with each other at different levels of interactions. At various times, I can choose to listen or to disengage. I can also choose to incorporate pieces of information into my own systems of meaning.

Our interactions or conversations with media work in similar ways. Conversations with the media cannot be clarified or negotiated. In everyday conversations, meanings are forever up for grabs. As active participants, we can ask for clarification, debate the viability of holding a particular perspective, and so on. But we can only guess at what might be the intended messages that exist behind the media images. As Baudrillard (1985) points out, there are few public spaces for providing a response to media information: "Power belongs to him [sic] who gives and to whom no return can be made" (p. 578).

In my (Hoskins) earlier description of reading a newspaper, there were few opportunities for responses (apart from discussing it with passengers seated near me) to these articles. Taking a rather pessimistic approach to the proliferation of media, Baudrillard (1985) claims that the current media explosion means that we are not only unable to respond to media but that, in North America, we are no longer able to study human behavior without also addressing the media: ". . . we will never in the future be able to separate reality from its statistical, simulative projection in the media, a state of suspense and definitive uncertainty about reality" (p. 580). This dialectical process of art imitating life and life imitating art raises questions of authenticity, but perhaps even more troublesome is the difficulty in determining the image from the thing itself.

The abundance of simulacra[2] (images with no referential object) calls into question the very nature of what is real and what is simulated. Uncertainty and its accompanying sidekick, anxiety, do not always result from an existential unknowing but rather have their seeds in a ground that is abundant with an excess of simulated "realities."

What are particularly problematic about this abundance of information are the values that frame and orchestrate the production of knowledge. The issue of whose interests are being served by presenting some knowledges and not others is highly contentious among feminist scholars (for example, Bordo, 1993; Faludi, 1991; hooks, 1984, 1994). For example, what versions of selfhood and everyday life are being produced, by whom, and for what purposes? Chomsky (2003) points out that media is not the least bit interested in creating healthy moral climates. Profit is the bottom line, not healthy environments.

Motives, therefore, behind media images, particularly in the fashion industry, are exclusively financially driven. In North America the growth of giant multinational media corporations, in particular, Time Warner and America Online, means that unelected business tycoons, not political leaders, hold enormous power (Giddens, 2000). With economic gains as their primary goals, news can be commodified in order to sell advertising and promote certain forms of ideology (for example, social, cultural, and political modes of thought). Given the demographics of multinational corporations (mainly males), input from those who are marginalized, in this case, women, is not even an option. For example, "women now hold 15.7 percent of corporate officer positions at large U.S companies" (The Washington Post, 11/19/2002). Furthermore, "There are nine women heading up the nation's largest 1,000 companies and 1.2 percent women chief executives running Fortune

500 companies (The New York Times, 01/13/2002). Regardless of whether or not having more women in positions of power would change the current state of affairs, one can only hope that through increased representation and recognition of diversity in major corporations, human values such as inclusion, equity, and social justice may co-exist alongside profit agendas.

Despite the lack of diversity among those in positions of influence in corporations, the proliferation of communication technologies, has exposed people to endless possibilities for constructing a life. This could be a liberating phenomenon. But instead, certain segments of the population find this "abundance of choice phenomenon" to be overwhelming and debilitating.

Many of the participants in our study expressed ambivalence about their capacity to choose; some believed there were too many choices in some areas such as careers and changing behaviors, whereas others felt there was little flexibility in what was expected of them as women. Indecision was prevalent in all of our conversations with girls. The reluctance to make choices regarding careers, what to eat, what to actually do with their spare time, and whether or not to remain with old friends or reach out to new ones, became common themes across all of our participant stories.

CACOPHONY OF CHOICES:
TO CHOOSE OR NOT TO CHOOSE

At no other time has there been such a multiplicity of signifiers (signs, symbols, images, metaphors, and so on) for constructing an identity. In the past, the church, state, and family were the most prevalent sources of the significant influences for constructing an identity for oneself. Values, ethics, principles, and guidelines for living a life were usually gleaned from local sources that existed in close proximity (Bellah, Madsen, Sullivan, Swidler, & Tipton, 1996; Giddens, 1991). Today, primarily due to the proliferation of communication technologies, influences arise from locations far beyond whatever could have been imagined in the past. For many young people, such a multitude of influences and, in turn, choices, can be highly problematic. Philosopher Mark Kingwell (2000) writes of the "cacophony of signals" that puts young people in the midst of constant pressure. While today's youth are rich in possibility, he argues that they are also "the test cases of a new task: that of finding meaningful roles to occupy in a complex global world where consumer choices loom larger than ethical ones, where brand loyalty counts for more than political fealty, where purely personal projects of comfort and success seem to push all other forms of value to one side" (p. 160).

This theme of too many mixed messages was affirmed by the girls in our research project to the point that many of them expressed difficulty in exercising their own sense of agency. It was as if they were suspended in time. Some of our participants spoke at length about their lost time while they were too sick to attend school and go out with friends. It seems they were suspended in time while determining how to proceed with their lives.

Frozen autonomy (Giddens, 2000) is often experienced by those struggling with addictive behaviors where what initially begins as a choice no longer becomes a chosen act. We also learned from our participants that that there was a desire on their part to extend their adolescence, thus in another sense, suspending development.

But how does choice in media contexts affect girls' identity challenges and, in turn, their lifespace? Biologist Humberto Maturana and psychologist Franscisco Varela (1987) have written extensively on the issue of nature versus nurture. Autopoesis (the ability for a person to be self-determining) positions choice or agency as not only structurally determined (biologically inherited) and socially free but also as needing to "structurally couple" with the environment. In other words, we are not entirely free to choose because, as relational beings, we can only construct identities in concert with the environment. But this process is not unidirectional. It is dialectical in that each person interacts with his or her environment, and such environments can actually change the structure of the person.

The idea of memes, not genes, is an important and useful concept when thinking about how people become socialized to act in a certain way. Memes are the repetitive social processes that are passed on from one generation to the next. Memes sneak into a person's developmental processes in the same way that genes work dynamically to shape a person's structure. Often they nestle into habitual behaviors that become taken for granted. Repetitive acts, like genetic processes, are what keep certain memes alive.

Conversely, disruption can render memetic actions obsolete. But this does not mean that memes and/or genes *cause* behavior. It is much more complex than that. Hayek (1979) reminds us that identity consists of a "dynamic and individualized coalition of (1) genetic or biological inheritance, (2) socially transmitted rules (most of which are tacit and prohibitive), and (3) only a thin layer of rules [that are] deliberately adopted or modified to serve known purposes (as cited in Mahoney, 1991, p. 136).

Hayek, along with several other important developmentalists such as Piaget and Freud, was theorizing in a different time, before the proliferation of television, computers, and other communication technologies. This last point about a "thin layer of rules" may not be so thin as formerly believed. It is this layering of rules that needs to be more fully understood if we are to begin to understand gender relations. Why are these rules adopted by some and not others? For what purposes were the rules constructed? Who made up the rules in the first place and under what kind of social conditions?

Foucault (1972) has some responses to these questions. Rules, he argues, are made up by those who are members of the "ruling apparatus:" those people who have privileged positions in society meaning, in many cases, a certain amount of wealth and power. In patriarchal societies, this usually translates to upholding male interests.

Traditions, customs, and habitual behaviors are all memes that are not natural but inventions created by societies when needed. The term *traditional* is often used to imply the way things are supposed to be. Giddens (2000) points out, though, that the problem with traditions is that many believe that there is stored up wisdom when, in fact, many traditions were created in order to support the ruling class. These memes and their accompanying rules usually have negative material and spiritual consequences for those who are marginalized, such as women and children.

This is not to suggest that all traditions are bad and should be abandoned; rather, it is to point out that we need to be wary of debates that position traditions as the truth and other alternative ways of living as unnatural. When it comes to examining the options for women in society, this kind of awareness is critical if change is to occur. Allocation of dollars for day care, women's health, and welfare have traditionally affected women's material lives more than men's. Currently, in British Columbia, for example, corporate interests appear to receive more tax breaks while programs that directly affect women's lives are being cut. Women still make up less than 20 percent of those who make decisions about the quality of their lives. Just 62 of 299 federal members of parliament in Canada are women. In addition, only 36 of the 102 senators in Canada are women (Canada's Parliament, n.d.). According to the United Nations Economic Commission for Europe (n.d.), in Canada, the gender breakdown for legislators, senior officials, and managers are as follows: 65% men and 35% women. Furthermore, in Canada, the annual average earnings for women are only 70% of that of men.

SHOPPING FOR SUBJECTIVITIES

With such limited influence in decision-making bodies, how can girls enter into debates about women's role in society? Without equal representation in governing bodies, it is argued that male interests will dominate public policy. Such influences also dominate media and the kinds of choices that are presented to girls on a daily basis. Given such a lack of representation, how do girls even know about available choices? Choosing an identity is not a one-way street. Instead, it is a dialectical process that moves between societal expectations and individual agency. Recruitment into certain discourses and the capacity to exercise choice interact.

Althusser (1971) claims that people are actively recruited into certain identities for a variety of reasons. It is as if someone calls out, "Hey you!" and a person answers by imitating certain behaviors, dress codes, right down to ways of walking and talking. Adolescents can shop for identities by joining certain sub-groups in their high schools and local communities. Some join because of default (no other clubs will accept them), while others have more options to choose from. In any case, all groups have these codes and rules for behavior, some more explicit than others.

But the idea that identities can be purchased, not only chosen, comes from the increase in consumerism in North American society. Messages are delivered via communication technologies that convince people that everything essential in life can be bought. If you are not born with significant characteristics (physical or psychological), it is all right because you can shop for them.

Empty selves, according to Cushman (1990), can be filled by merely purchasing more "objects" to construct a self. But what if the only available "products" on the shelves are generic brands and not the real thing? What if the image has no referential substance? Most, if not all, of the girls we interviewed were fully aware of how images, especially those in fashion magazines, had no resemblance to anyone in the real world. They knew that images were digitally manipulated to project an image almost beyond belief. Interestingly, although they knew this, it did not prevent them from using such images for goals for themselves.

> I know like the pictures of the models . . . in magazines aren't real, their bodies are totally modified and everything, just to look good but it does affect me a lot because whenever I look through a magazine with a guy or something, they always pick the skinniest one. Well, that's the hottest one obviously. So, it does trigger me a little bit just thinking . . . well, I have to become that skinny to look that good. Or I have to be that skinny to wear those kind of clothes or something like that. That really bothers me!

And another participant echoes these same concerns:

> I think that definitely the media has played a part in my viewpoint and I think the media plays a part in a lot [of people's viewpoints] because, you know, it's everywhere, and you can't necessarily get away from it. Take models for instance, yeah, it's just really unhealthy and it's almost as though they put out these unrealistic ideals that they expect everyone to match but when, in truth, realistically, I mean, you're going to end up killing yourself trying to. And I just don't feel that that is something the world should be projecting. But . . . so I have very mixed opinions about the media.

Through our study of media we found that although there appears to be an abundance of symbols and signifiers for how to live one's life, there are still narrowly defined measures for having a socially acceptable female body.

MANUFACTURING ENVY

While girls believe they can shop for identities, advertisers are also busy orchestrating an emotional experience of discontent. Kingwell (1998) writes about how the media manufactures discontent for a particular purpose, which is to advance the practice of convincing people that they can buy happiness. Advertisers believe this to be true and have developed rationales and protocols for working within this perspective. Advertising works for the following reasons.

First, we measure ourselves against proximate others (proximate because distance makes the heart grow less envious). This is an important concept and one that the participants in our study confirmed. If the magazine images were too unrealistic, if there was no possibility that they could look like them, then they were rejected outright. In order for the ads to work, they had to have some reference to something familiar in their own lives.

Second, advertising works by playing on unavailability: the key is that the viewer does not possess the product. All of the girls we interviewed believed that the ideal body was just beyond their reach.

Third, desire is *created* through advertising, not *discovered*. There is no intrinsic desire embedded within the psyches of individuals; rather, it is socially constructed through the imagination of those in the advertisement business.

Fourth, paradoxically, advertising is not about contributing to the overall well-being of society but, instead, is about creating a state of discontent and anxiety that will promote consumerism, not other, more humanitarian kinds of goals.

All of these processes are not commonly understood by the general population. Advertisers basically work behind our backs to create conditions that are conducive to promoting their products. According to Baudrillard (1985), we have now become a society comprised of "cultural dopes" who mindlessly accept images without question. This is one perspective. Conversely, some argue that we have become media literate and are now able to discern underlying messages that may be harmful. What we discovered in our research is that even when girls knowingly read magazines and subjected themselves to the barrage of advertising sandwiched between their favorite television shows and tucked between articles about fashion and teen culture, they still found themselves envying the bodies and lifestyles represented.

> It [media] doesn't make you feel good. All of my life I've been a little bit chubby. And I always wanted to be one of those thin models, not super thin. I just wanted to be healthy looking and that's how they make it look. They don't show normal people . . . and just like guys even know. But it seems like most guys . . . that's all they want. They want big boobs, and skinny.

One of the areas we are currently pursuing is the appropriation of human values in order to sell products. For example, KIA, the "car that cares" and State Farm Insurance, "like a good neighbor," are well known examples. Companies as well as products themselves are also portrayed to have humanistic values, not capitalistic ends. This usurping of human values can be easily detected by those who pay attention to the underlying messages. The danger of assigning human characteristics to inanimate objects is that the reverse can too readily happen where people become objectified and dehumanized. Deeper knowledge of how these kinds of tactics filter down to influence self-system, however, needs more research. In the meantime, how can practitioners proceed when working with the mediated worlds of girls?

ORIENTATING QUESTIONS

What we have presented in this chapter is a glimpse of some of the complexities of understanding mediated selves in a consumer society. *Media relations* is a term we use to refer to the process a person engages in when he or she reads culture through a variety of media texts. It emphasizes the constitutive aspects of scripting oneself into an identity and, at the same time, being scripted by the text. If this concept of media relations is kept at the forefront of our consciousness about how media interacts with constructing a self, then we, as practitioners, can avoid the pitfalls of thinking we can objectively know another person's lifespace. We will also be better equipped to understand how girls make meaning of cultural symbols in relation to their own identities.

There are no set skills when working with the mediated environments of girls. Instead, there are orienting questions that can assist practitioners to navigate their way through many complex and contradictory signs and signifiers. First, in order to orient oneself to mediated environments, it is important as practitioners to raise our own consciousness. There are ways to interpret popular culture, particularly when using a gender focus while reading. We like to think of the process of zooming in on the micro-details of story to panning back to focus on how the story is told within a mosaic of layers of cultural norms and expectations. This same process of zooming in and panning out can be used when conversing with girls. Important orienting questions for practitioners to be mindful of are: How is this story situated within a landscape of gender relations? What does this story imply about the role of women in society? How are these stories positioned among other stories? What overall themes and scripts are being perpetuated about women's lives?

Second, another way of orienting ourselves is to challenge our own assumptions. To give a concrete example from my (Hoskins) own life (actually more of a confessional tale), I was recently surprised by my own lack of gender awareness. It happened while I was sitting in a restaurant, observing a male and female having lunch. The woman appeared to be in her late 50s or early 60s, and the male was about 35 years old. My initial thought was that they were a nice mother and son having lunch together–it even made me think of my own sons and how much I missed having that kind of time with them. When she began to stroke his hair and he, in response, held her hand, I soon realized that they were a romantic couple, not mother and son. My first reaction was to assume she was "looking after him" and must have money. Why else would such a young, nice looking man be with her? I felt sorry for her as it would just be a matter of time until she was abandoned, I assumed. I also felt a certain amount of disdain towards her, at one moment feeling pity for her and, at the next, disgust at how she had lowered herself to that level.

But would these mixed feelings of pity and disdain be felt if this was an older man with a younger woman? Why was I not able to catch my own prejudices in the making and transform them into more enlightened reactions? In one fell swoop of emotional responses, I colluded with the status quo that supports attitudes of respect and admiration for mature men courting younger women and condemns older women who "prey" on younger men. There is even a derogatory term for such women: cougars. My purpose for including this brief description is to highlight the importance for practitioners to engage in their own ongoing struggles with changing attitudes towards gender stereotypes, to catch ourselves when we are mindlessly going along with the traditional, patriarchal flow.

Third, we need to continue to refine and elaborate our meaning-making questions so that we can be sensitive to the individual differences that arise when working with the intersections between media and the self. Cultural artifacts such as music, movies, icons, and images are open to unique interpretations as well as shared understandings. If we take a meaning-making orientation we can ask: When you listen to that kind of music what does it bring forth in you? What is your experience of reading fashion magazines? What do you think is the intent of the advertiser when certain images are used? When you are feeling down about yourself, where do you think these feelings come from?

A final way of orienting ourselves as practitioners is to instill hopefulness about the ability to resist harmful media images. We cannot just throw up our hands in despair. A physician once said to us that fighting the media is like trying to win a nuclear war with a pea shooter. But passively accepting negative media images is not the answer. We need to create opportunities for dialogue, resistance, and advocacy.

One of our students, for example, was upset about a radio advertisement that was sexist in its approach to dieting behaviors. Together we successfully lobbied for its removal. Although these are small acts of protest and resistance, they are still a beginning in fostering consciousness about how media shapes women's lives, and how women respond to such processes.

In summary, when working with adolescent girls' identity challenges, we need to pay attention to how media impacts the ways in which they describe their unique lifespace. Although many argue that there is a multitude of choices for constructing a female identity in today's society, others contend such choices are simulacra, not real or even viable models for living a life. The orienting questions above provide a framework for dialoging with girls about their relation to media and the meanings that they participate in co-creating. Media, from our perspective, is no longer an add-on or background noise—it has now become an influencing current that runs through our lives. Much can be learned from working relationally with girls in order to understand the influence of media on constructing an identity.

NOTES

1. All excerpts are taken from the Daily Mail, October 17th, 2003.
2. Simulacra, defined as "copies without originals," (Lather, 1993) suggests we have moved from a culture of representations to one of images, which masks the absence of referential finalities. Contending we have entered a televisual age where the image has been confused with reality, some cultural theorists argue we are in an age of hyperreality where reality is no longer what it used to be (Baudrillard, 1983; Lyotard, 1984). Along a similar theme, Denzin (1991) refers to the use of codes lacking the same kinds of representations.

REFERENCES

Althusser, L. (1971). *Lenin and philosophy and other essays.* London: New Left Books.
Barker, S. B., Barker, R. T., Dawson, K. S., & Knisely, J. S. (1997). The use of the Family Life Space Diagram in establishing inter-connectedness: A preliminary study of sexual abuse survivors, their significant others, and pets. *Individual Psychology, 53,* 435-450.
Baudrillard, J. (1983). *Simulations.* New York: Semiotext(e).
Baudrillard, J. (1985). The masses: The implosion of the social in the media. *New Literary History, 16,* 577-589.
Bellah, R. N., Madsen, R., Sullivan, W. M., Swidler, A., & Tipton, S. M. (1996). *Habits of the heart: Individualism and commitment in American life.* Berkeley, CA: University of California Press.

Bordo, S. (1993). *Unbearable weight: Feminism, western culture, and the body.* Berkeley, CA: University of California Press.

Brumberg, J. (1997). *The body project.* New York: Random House.

Canada's Parliament (n.d.). *Women in the Senate.* Retrieved November 14, 2003, From http://www.parl.gc.ca/common/senmemb/senate/isenator.asp?sortord=W&Language=E

Chomsky, N. (2003). Power and terror: Post 9/11 talks and interviews. New York: Seven Stories Press.

Cushman, P. (1990). Why the self is empty: Toward a historically situated psychology. *American Psychologist, 45*(5), 599-611.

Daily Mail, Friday, October 17, 2003. London, England.

Denzin, N. (1991). Empiricist cultural studies in America: A deconstructive reading. *Current Perspectives in Social Theory, 11,* 17-39.

Faludi, S. (1991). *Backlash: The undeclared war against American women.* New York: Doubleday.

Foucault, M. (1972). *The archaeology of knowledge and the discourse on language.* New York: Harper & Row.

Gergen, K. (1991). *The saturated self.* New York: Basic Books.

Gergen, K. (1996). Technology and the self: From the essential to the sublime. In D. Grodin & T. Lindlof (Eds.), *Constructing the self in a mediated world* (127-140). Thousand Oaks, CA: Sage Publications.

Gibson, J. (2000). A good hearing? An application of the life space interview in residential child care. *Child Care in Practice, 6,* 39-52.

Giddens, A. (1991). *Modernity and self-identity: Self and society in the late modern age.* Stanford, CA: Stanford University Press.

Giddens, A. (2000). *Runaway world: How globalization is reshaping our lives.* New York: Routledge Press.

Grodin, D., & Lindlof, T. (Eds.) (1996). *Constructing the self in a mediated world.* Thousand Oaks, CA: Sage Publications.

Harré, R., & Gillett, G. (1994). *The discursive mind.* Thousand Oaks, CA: Sage Publications.

Hayek, F. A. (1979). *Law, legislation, and liberty: Rules and order.* (Vol. 1). Chicago: University of Chicago Press.

Hedelin, B. (2001). The meaning of depression from the life-world perspective of elderly women. *Issues in Mental Health Nursing, 22,* 401-420.

hooks, b. (1984). *Feminist theory from margin to center.* Boston, MA: South End Press.

hooks, b. (1994). *Outlaw culture: Resisting representations.* New York: Routledge.

Kingwell, M. (1998). *Better living: In pursuit of happiness from Plato to Prozac.* Toronto, ON: Penguin Books.

Kingwell, M. (2000). *The world we want: Virtue, vice, and the good citizen.* Toronto, Ontario: Penguin Books.

Krueger, M., & Stuart, C. (1999). Context and competence in work with children and youth. *Child & Youth Care Forum, 28,* 195-204.

Larson, R., & Richards, M. J. (1989). Introduction: The changing life space of early adolescence. *Journal of Youth & Adolescence, 18,* 501-509.

Lather, P. (1993). Fertile obsession: Validity after poststructuralism. *Sociological Quarterly, 34*, 673-693.

Lewin, K. (1936). *Principles of topological psychology.* New York: McGraw-Hill.

Lewin, K. (1954). Behavior and development as a function of the total situation. In L. Carmichael (Ed.), *Manual of child psychology* (2nd ed., pp. 918-970). New York: Wiley.

Lyotard, J. (1984). *The postmodern condition.* Minneapolis, MN: University of Minnesota Press.

Mahoney, M. J. (1991). *Human change processes: The scientific foundations of psychotherapy.* New York: Basic Books.

Maturana, H. R., & Varela, F. J. (1987). *The tree of knowledge.* London: Shambhala.

Motswin, D. (1980). *Life space approach to the study and treatment of a family.* Washington, DC: Catholic University of America.

New York Times (2002, January 13). Retrieved August 2, 2004, from http://www.ceogo.com/CEOFACTS/DEMOGRAPHICS/

Oyserman, D., & Swim, J. K. (2001). Stigma: An insider's view. *Journal of Social Issues, 57*, 1-14.

Redl, F. (1982). Child care work. *Journal of Child Care, 1*(2), 3-9.

Richards, M. J., & Larson, R. (1989). The life space and socialization of the self: Sex differences in the young adolescent. *Journal of Youth & Adolescence, 18*, 617-626.

Szymanksi, E. M. (1994). Transition: Life-span and life-space considerations for empowerment. *Exceptional Children, 60*, 402-410.

The Washington Post (2002, November 19). Retrieved August 2, 2004, from http://www.ceogo.com/CEOFACTS/DEMOGRAPHICS/

United Nations Economic Commission for Europe (n.d.). *Gender Statistics Database.* Retrieved November 14, 2003, from http://www.unece.org/stats/gender/web/database.htm

"It's an Acceptable Identity": Constructing "Girl" at the Intersections of Health, Media, and Meaning-Making

J. Nicole Little
Marie L. Hoskins

SUMMARY. This article explores the authors' critical reflections that arose while engaging in research with girls recovering from an eating disorder. The authors address issues related to media, consumerism, and identity construction. They emphasize that while there are no clear solutions to dilemmas facing girls in North American culture, researchers and practitioners can co-create space with girls where gendered issues are made explicit. Their holistic framework for working with girls does not imply a neutral approach; rather, they aim to honor the complexity of gendered narratives and critically reflect on their implications for practice. *[Article copies available for a fee from The Haworth Document Delivery Service: 1-800-HAWORTH. E-mail address: <docdelivery@haworthpress.com> Website: <http://www.HaworthPress.com> © 2004 by The Haworth Press, Inc. All rights reserved.]*

J. Nicole Little, MA (in progress), is affiliated with the School of Child and Youth Care, Faculty of Human and Social Development, University of Victoria. Marie L. Hoskins, PhD, is Associate Professor, School of Child and Youth Care, Faculty of Human and Social Development, University of Victoria.

Address correspondence to: Dr. Marie L. Hoskins, School of Child and Youth Care, Faculty of Human and Social Development, University of Victoria, Box 1700, Victoria, BC, V8W 2Y2, Canada (E-mail: mhoskins@uvic.ca)

The study was made possible by the generous funding of the Social Sciences and Humanities Council (SSHRC).

[Haworth co-indexing entry note]: "'It's an Acceptable Identity': Constructing 'Girl' at the Intersections of Health, Media, and Meaning-Making." Little, J. Nicole, and Marie L. Hoskins. Co-published simultaneously in *Child & Youth Services* (The Haworth Press, Inc.) Vol. 26, No. 2, 2004, pp. 75-93; and: *Working Relationally with Girls: Complex Lives/Complex Identities* (ed: Marie L. Hoskins, and Sibylle Artz) The Haworth Press, Inc., 2004, pp. 75-93. Single or multiple copies of this article are available for a fee from The Haworth Document Delivery Service [1-800-HAWORTH, 9:00 a.m. - 5:00 p.m. (EST). E-mail address: docdelivery@haworthpress.com].

Available online at http://www.haworthpress.com/web/CYS
Digital Object Identifier: 10.1300/J024v26n02_05

KEYWORDS. Identity development, feminism, consumerism, adolescent girls, eating disorders, youthwork, youth work

It takes a lot of courage to be a girl. This is not a romantic statement. In a North American context, we see the girls with whom we work grappling with a complex, media-saturated world that does not easily accept those who fall outside the often rigid scripts of gender and gendered expectations. How then do these girls make sense of themselves, their relationships, and their worlds in a way that allows them to express their multiple selves in prescriptive social and gendered categories? The chapter explores the authors' critical reflections[1] about working with girls.[2] We offer neither linear solutions nor clear-cut examples; rather, we follow the lead of girls we have worked with in terms of opening dialogue regarding ambiguity and contradictions. Like many other human service practitioners, we have often wished for a simplified approach to addressing some of the most pressing and relentless and, in some cases, potentially dangerous issues facing girls: negotiating relationships (both platonic and intimate), disordered body image and disordered eating, negotiating media, sense of self, and "meaning-making." This chapter explores the "meaning-making" girls engage in when articulating identity processes. Complicating this process is that our "consultants"[3] are in the midst of the health challenge of disordered eating in a world that is dominated by consumerism. Given the paradoxical messages reflected in the media and the contradictions inherent in a multiple selves perspective, we present some of the challenges in paying attention to the many layers of girls' identities. We believe that approaching girls with a holistic framework is essential in understanding the intersections of "meaning-making," specifically for understanding how gender is taken up. A holistic framework, however, does not imply a neutral approach; rather, we aim to take up complexity of gendered narratives and critically reflect on their implications for thinking about practice with girls.

SKETCHING THE TOPOGRAPHY

Just when we think we may have "it" when addressing the needs of girls, personal narratives create new questions and directions:

I pick up a copy of *Sassy* magazine and read it cover to cover, then toss it in the trash. I really can't believe, looking at the beautiful, thin, white models and the articles about finding the right boyfriend, that it masquerades as some kind of alternative teen magazine, that it purports to be profeminist [*sic*], pro-girl, pro-intelligence. This is what it means to be an intelligent girl? Listening to bands with female members and wearing a more natural shade of lipstick? I feel like we've been forgotten, I feel like we're all dying of anorexia and heartbreak, and everyone-you-you just turn the other way. (Doza, 1995, p. 252)

Doza strikes into the heart of practitioners on two levels: one, she exposes the pain and contradictions of living as a teenage girl in a particular pocket of society, and she challenges adult practitioners to give space for her voice. In many respects, we feel like we know her personally. She is like many girls with whom we have worked who are angry and demand answers. She is what we wished many girls could have been: aware, political, and angry. She is also like ourselves, only born in a different generation. When we think of working with girls in this corner of North America, what do we view as essential and important? How do we work with the emerging gendered and consumed identities that are named "female adolescence"? And how does consumerism and sexism foreshadow our interventions with girls, and why do these constructs demand our attention?

We are two adult practitioners who have worked with girls in a variety of settings, and we grapple with these questions every day. Experiences such as consulting with girls about illness, health, and meaning and working in the moment with personal crisis and change have told us that we cannot apply a "one size fits all" therapeutic model. We are mindful that working with girls is much more than arbitrary application of "tools" taught in human service programs.[4] It is being *intentionally* therapeutic and *intentionally* aware of gender and sexism. This is more than "active listening" that we learn; it is a relational experience wherein we concurrently see and hear the individual and the context she is embedded in. More specifically, we have come to the realization that girls are shaping themselves in the midst of market identities, post-feminism, and a relentless, shrinking "ideal" body image. In working with girls, all three conditions intersect, bolstering each other and sometimes jostling for dominance in a girl's narrative of her self. As the girls in our research articulated their experiences, it became clear that their understanding and embodiment of gender and consumerism was often contradictory and paradoxical (see, for example, McLuhan, 1964). As the story of adolescence unfolds, we must ask ourselves what backgrounds are being drafted, what characters are girls including, and how do practitioners help in meaningful ways? The multiplicity of identities must be acknowledged if we are to understand the richness and complexity of adolescent girls' lives and subjective meanings of self. Equally important is the understanding of our role as human service practitioners in helping negotiate these intersectionalities.

HOW DOES ONE CONSTRUCT THE "SELF"?

We believe that girls do not come to us with fixed and static interpretations of themselves and their world. At the same time, we are cautious in announcing a wild optimism for unlimited variability in the construction(s) of self. Consumers are bombarded with slogans that implore, "Just do it," and we can now purchase bumper stickers that extol "Girl Power." A dissonance occurs, however, when one realizes that you cannot "just do it," because the boys won't let you play with them or particular social locations restrict the options for higher education and/or vocational training.

In my (Little) experience working in the field of sexual health, we champion (heterosexual) girls to "just do it" in the context of taking charge of their health (especially around condom use). Yet in doing so, we assume an equal playing ground on which they can "just do it." This minimizes the complexity of actually changing in a society that restricts choice for some but not others. The dissonance is further experienced through the materialization of what constitutes "girl power." Witness the corporate co-opting demonstrated by the Spice Girls. In fact, the Spice Girls, although long dispersed and no longer a hot commodity, may be perceived as an example of how marketing is played out under the guise of championing girlhood (Driscoll, 1999). This "girl power," however, is non-threatening in that it simply sells gender appropriate appearances and messages without reconstructing what it may mean to be female in this day and age. It reminds us of leftovers–the dish has all the same ingredients of sexism, colonialism, and infantilization, but it is served up in a shiny new container. How complex it is for girls and young women to decide what constitutes legitimate agency and power? As practitioners, we often assume to know and model what this legitimate agency is without critiquing how we carry forth sexist assumptions and practices.

We propose that the creation of the self, in this case for girls, is a complex negotiation of gendered scripts and subjective stages on which these scripts are performed. Girls who consult with us may have been told that girls can do anything, that the contemporary world is apt to say, "Gender no longer matters." After all, just reading the daily newspaper reassures us that girls are doing better in math, and movies such as *Bend it like Beckham* prove both culture and gender can be rendered neutral with enough lightheartedness. While girls may have a perceived freedom within an arena of choices (Hoskins, 1997), such choices are still the stuff of social expectations.

For example, Gergen (2001) asks, "Aren't we all, including you, whatever your identity, hostage to social conventions?" (p. 82). The metaphor of hostage is indeed powerful. If we accept this claim, how does it change our perspective on working with girls? To what are they held hostage to? And how do we "liberate" them, or is that even our job? Besides, did the women's movement in the seventies not already do that? In other words, what space are we responsible for co-creating with girls outside the dominant scripts that saturate our lives?

The metaphor of hostage, unfortunately, does fit well in an era of post 9/11 anxieties. We cannot deny that we have been impacted by a new reality, or new perspective of reality, in the aftermath of 9/11. The naming of such an event is neither meant to sensationalize panic nor trivialize the mourning and racism that individuals and communities endured; rather, we invite the reader to consider the new anxiety that has seized many North Americans and to contemplate the many levels on which the concept "hostage" can be considered. Although the definition of hostage provided by the *Concise Oxford Dictionary*, "Person[s] seized or held as security for fulfillment of a condition" (Thompson, 1995, p. 656) may appear counter to a traditional academic discourses of a strengths-based or humanist perspective, we implore readers to consider gender as a tangible and embodied construct that can no longer be ignored.

For example, the predominant theory we see across human service professions is "active listening," which translates into practice as "hug them harder." Yet, listening is not a neutral exercise. It actively entangles our own constructions of gender and professional expectations of what constitutes safe space for the stories of girls. We extol the virtues of "voice" and, as feminists, we do not deny that girls have been silenced. What is problematic for us is that raising voice is not necessarily parallel to addressing the context in which that voice is encouraged to speak out. The idea that because we care for and listen to the youth we work with, and may care more than other people in their lives, does not render the oppressive paradigms in which they live invalid or invisible. We cannot individually hug away sexism and associated violence. In fact, in denying the importance of the previous two realities, we too are taken hostage, but compliantly.

The hostage taker is both a visible and invisible tether on the potential of girls. For example, the "social convention" that Gergen (2001) refers to can be construed in North America as a consumer culture. Social convention in this context includes the varied visual types of media, hyper-communication modes, and a bombardment of images on any available surface, be it ice on a rink or highway billboards, high school year books, or airport baggage claims. The invisible social conventions then become the internal process of making an identity out of the limited choices that abound in these different forms. Much has been written about the relationships and effects of media on girls' self-esteem and understanding.[5] Less attention, however, has been directed at how to work with girls who identify as consumers and see consuming as an inherent component to "being" a girl. Or, should we say, *the right kind of girl.* Hence, we see girls as hostage to capitalism and what Hoskins (see Hoskins and Mathieson, this volume) has coined: Its ensuing manufacturing of envy.

MANUFACTURING ENVY

The envy aspect is crucial in the taking up of gendered scripts. Heterosexist indoctrination has prompted many practitioners to consider this envy in the context of competition for male attention, and we do not deny that girls may experience ruptures in their relationships with each other based on pursuit of intimate (heterosexual) relationships. Artz's (1997) research with girls supports this perspective and she states: "Friendships with girls were characterized by shifts from enemy to friend and back again, and revolved around competition for male attention" (p. 27). In fact, one conflict detailed by one of our participants in a recent inquiry describes this very idea (also see Hoskins & Mathieson, this volume). Yet the majority of envy and assessment, according to the girls who were consultants in our study, is not primarily about male attention. The girls we consulted clearly articulated that such envy manifested in assessment of other girls. For example, one girl commented, "Oh, there's always the comparing. That's always the biggest conflict and it's huge. You can . . . when you're anorexic you can compare your bestest [*sic*] friend and be jealous of her and love her at the same time."

We wonder if this lack of collective agreement about to whom girls are performing gender for (other girls or boys) speaks to the complexity of defining the audience of gender. Another girl, when asked if there was competition between girls, told us,

> Yeah, because I used to always think–not tell her–but I'd always feel, like, "Oh, she's way thinner than me." Yeah, I think they totally do [compare each other]. Like, they have, like, bigger boobs and she's thinner and whatever. Or she's better than me at this but I think guys do that too. I see that with my brother. Like, "I'm more muscular than this guy." But I think with girls it's a bit more painful because you can sort of lift weights to get more muscular, with girls you might sort of, like, die.

Even as adult interviewers, we retrospectively caught ourselves speaking in language ripe with envious overtones when conveying stories. Such examples include self-deprecating comments about our own body size and/or appetites and expressions tinged with jealousy when speaking of other women's eating habits. Clearly, the manufacturing of envy is neither confined to adolescents nor to those with eating disorders. In fact, consumerism as an ideology would not be successful if not for its promotion of competition, the "keeping up with the Jones" mentality that influences North American consumption. By not questioning this phenonenomen, we exhaust ourselves running a race that has no finish line, essentially, a race that cannot be won. The question that so many practitioners may be asking is "Well, what is the point?" Yet precisely because there is no singular "point" of entry or departure when discussing identity, consumerism and gender is why we need to be ever vigilant about the socially constructed intersections girls contend with.

CONTESTED (MARKET) PLACES AND SPACES

While we acknowledge our own grappling with gender as adult women, we also recognize that girls live in a unique place as adolescents. By "place" we are referring to the location they hold in relation to social conventions and social relationships. Given that "adolescent girls grapple with their development as women amidst . . . contradictions, [and] they frequently pay harsh social and psychological consequences"

(Mensinger, 2001, p. 418), it is no surprise that "adolescent identity is thus treated as a practical accomplishment achieved through a contradictory discourse mediated by social texts that include commercial magazines" (Currie, 1999, p. 113). How do we, as practitioners, acknowledge this contradictory existence? Are the contradictions we may experience as adult women comparable to those of girls? Have we lived with paradoxical gender messages for so long that they are no longer glaringly apparent, hence, less urgent in our everyday routines? The "place" girls occupy is also recognized as a socially constructed period of time.

If we agree with Steinberg (2002), who argues that "the way in which we divide the life cycle into stages, drawing a boundary between childhood and adolescence, for example, is nothing more than a reflection of the political, economic, and social circumstances in which we live" (p. 15), it follows that "female adolescence" is seen as a socially constructed *marketplace*. It must be noted, however, that this is not a universal phenomenon. Wald (1998) illuminates this:

> Acquiring its meaning, like the signifier *woman,* within the context of specific discursive regimes, *girlhood* is not a universal component of female experience; rather, the term implies very specific practices and discourses about female sexuality, women's cultural-political agency, and women's social location. (p. 591, emphasis in original)

Specific practices such as shopping, body modification, and expressions of heterosexual desire could all be considered "normal" in the space of female adolescence. This contextualized marketplace offers for its wares a limited variety of narratives. Since identity narratives cannot be convincingly isolated from other social variables, commodities that bolster the visibility and legitimacy of such narratives are also available. Currie (1994) also asserts that manufacturers' strength is their ability to manipulate commodities that are "solutions that entail lifestyle rather than social and political change" (p. 103).

RESEARCHER REFLEXIVITY

We reflected on our own experiences of girlhood and consuming by posing the question: "What was the first product bought and did it support 'appropriate' gender displays?" An example is when I (Little) at age 6 bought a hair clip with my best friend, each clip with a silk flower attached. While we understood ourselves to be girls long before this pivotal purchase, we also amplified this girlness by striking poses with our new hair clips, tossing our hair and giggling. This was not considered unusual and was, in fact, encouraged by the sales clerk. If we were to change this scenario and replace the girls with boys, some may comment it would border on a ridiculous parody. And even though we know that gender is a socialization experience, when we still continue to accept such socialization as normal we condone the commodification of girls and girlhood.

For example, the reader may be asking: "What's so terrible? A harmless hairclip! Relax!" But does the reader have the same reaction to lingerie chains marketing an array of sexy underwear to girls between 10-13 years of age? Is this what we meant by empowering girls? You can choose bikini or thong cut. Is that what we meant by choice? Why is the mass marketing we are under siege from only blamed in the context of body images and not in the context of bodily experiences? For example, the hair clip could be construed as a symbol of feminine beauty; hence, the body image associated with its sale is based on enhancement. The body, however, is experienced pejoratively as it has now experienced lacking a material object deemed necessary. Parents may experience this on an annual basis with the back to school gluttony and the real, felt distress by girls denied some "necessary" brand name or item. This is where the hostage taking of our girls by capitalism is played out. It is not a single, dramatic event but rather, a series of abductions so subtle that we do not address them. Gergen (2001) reflects: "To live in a story of the body that is different from another's can render an impasse of understanding" (p. 74), and it is the act of consuming that creates the impasse in the first place. The impasse is then maintained through the constant quest for enhancement and cycled through periods of assessment and comparison.

NEGOTIATING GENDERED IDENTITIES

What we are interested in is how girls negotiate this impasse. Specifically, how is gender taken up and made true for self or other girls? Since the authors agree that gender cannot be discarded (after all, how do you step outside your skin?), how do girls take up stories to explain themselves as people, as girls, and as consumers? Currie (2001) articulates this well:

> While cultural critics may celebrate [magazine] texts as the site of struggle and reader resistance, in this study girls found ontological security and a sense of belonging in magazine constructions. For us, "belonging" is not simply about membership through similarity between the experienced and the constructed world of adolescence, however. Rather membership occurs when it imports "ownership" of the subject position constructed by the text. Ownership is not simply a result of relevance, as identified through a study of magazine content: ownership comes when the reader actively takes up the subjective position offered by the text. (pp. 265-266)

As Currie and many of our participants point out, media does not "make" girls anorexic, feminine, and so forth. Rather, it interacts with readers and negotiates ownership of such images. In doing so, girls feel themselves to be making an agentic choice despite this being made in the context of "constrained agency" (O'Brien Hallstein, 1999). The question for us is the benefits and detriments of exploring this constrained choice with girls. My (Little) mother sagely stated once: "You can't be the demolition crew without ensuring a clean up crew," meaning, of course, we cannot destroy a sense of reality without offering a context in which to re-create a new (and more intentional) reality. Even as adults, we become overwhelmed with the lack of truly liberating roles to take up. Do we have the right to shine the spotlight on the structural limitations of being a girl? Or does *not* asking this question imply a colonialist mindset (i.e., we must "save" the so-called ignorant)? In fact, many girls agree that identities are pre-packaged, especially those that centre on disordered eating. As one consultant reflected:

> Once you have it [an eating disorder], it's safe; I know that, like for me, now it's safe because I know. What makes women . . . [gravitate toward disordered eating] . . . okay, I'm just going to say I don't know the answer to that so I'm just, like, maybe it's accepted. Like, it's an acceptable identity. I'm just trying to think about media now and like connecting it back and everything like that. And it's, it's an identity that's kind of nourished by our society. I don't know what makes it attractive because once you have it, its not attractive at all.

The manifestation of an eating disorder moves away from individual, intrapsyche pathology to an off-the-rack, complete outfit ready for public view, with the same girl stating: "I have a whole identity from my eating disorder. It gives me things to do, it gives me ways to act, and people know me as [name], the one with the eating disorder." Her emphasis on what constitutes acceptable girl identities is important to consider as practitioners working with girls from all sorts of contexts. If the contextual realities of girls are infinite, why are acceptable identities so limited? What tension does this produce for girls trying to write a new story of their life, namely adolescence and young adulthood?

CONSULTING THE MEDIA EXPERTS

In our conversations with girls, they have been clear that they are neither media dupes nor patriarch's pawns. They have the technology, the lingo, and the media savvy to articulate what is wrong with the images that bombard them. Furthermore, girls we have consulted also recognize these images, specifically, images of women in advertisements, to be unrealistic and exploitive. Also, the girls demonstrated that they see some images out of context. One girl, when asked what types of magazines promote underweight models, stated: "All of them. Even if it's, like, some gardening magazine [laughter] they have, like, this woman who's, like, stick skinny." At the same time, conversations demonstrate a tension between parodying female scripts and embodying them. Although an image of a drag queen may evoke an "over the top-can't be real" reaction, can we truly parody gender at the "girl" level where such parody may not be understood by others? What of parody that is hyper-sexualized? Is this understood by those socialized in a sexist world?

Wald (1998), for example, is highly critical of what is referred to as transgressive gender play. By this she refers to the ultra-feminine manifestations often seen in contemporary rock music. Whether this is true parody or post-modern money-making, we must be aware of who gets to engage in this practice. Wald reminds us that the levying of social penalties is a real and lived experience for those stepping outside of gender and that it is a relative privilege to do so unscathed. The narrow performance of gender, then, whether motivated by tradition or mockery, remains a tether on the potential of girls.

I [Little] often catch myself musing: "Can't girls see sexism unfolding in all aspects of their stories?" Yet because different generational and socio-contextual realities inform our understanding of sexism, the reactions to and rationalization of sexist examples also differ. This reaction also contradicts the girls' assertion that competition is for oneself against other girls and has nothing to do with boys. For example, in one conversation, a consultant described a crisis point in a friendship when her friend began dating a boy who she had been interested in for over a year. All blame was assigned to the female friend, and the boy occupied a neutral role on the wings. This was from the same young woman who told us that "I actually feel like a feminist saying this, like a women's libber but I think it's really at the fault of men, for putting women in their place all those years. I think it's just testosterone creating all the rules."

If this young woman occupied the true role of hostage of sexism, would she not revolt against her capture? Would she not choose to ally with her female friend and dismiss this classic, almost formula-like gendered triangle? Her rationale was that: "He's playing God." Hence she is operating on a conscious level within the parameters available, and her God metaphor lends a sense of omnipotence, of untouchable status. Like so many, she perpetrates the notion of heterosexual competition as individual honour, that somehow, her lack of success in this particular romantic pursuit renders her less than the so-called successful female friend. The hostage taker has informed her that her personal integrity (her honour) can only remain intact if she is desirable. Desirability and personal integrity, then, become an incestuous relative to sister competition.

Kate Bornstein, on the other hand, would see this young girl as a cult member, not a victim of a hostage taking. She states: "Gender is a cult. Membership in gender is not based on informed consent. There is no way out without people ridiculed and harassed. There is peer pressure that is brought to bear on everyone in this cult" (cited in Bell, 1993, p. 111). Cults, of course, inform behavior, roles, and relationships. Since cults normalize all aspects of their interactions and restrictions of their members, it is not a large stretch to apply this philosophy to gender. Furthermore, the word "cult" may raise eyebrows and quicken pulses, but we see this as an important aspect in announcing the urgency that is needed in addressing gender in the lives of girls. Issues of gender have been swallowed by politically correct rhetoric that essentially retains gender on a superficial level. Without moving to a deeper level of understanding and awareness, the status quo cult continues to rule.

So, how do we sound the alarm? hooks (2000) asserts:

> Women must begin the work of feminist reorganization with the understanding that we have all (irrespective of our race, sex, or class) acted in complicity with the existing oppressive system. We all need to make a conscious break with the system. Some of us

make this break sooner than others. The compassion we extend to ourselves, the recognition that our change in consciousness and action has been a process, must characterize our approach to those individuals who are politically unconscious. We cannot motivate them to join feminist struggle by asserting a political superiority that makes the movement just another oppressive hierarchy. (p. 164)

This quote was originally published in 1984 yet begs contemporary contemplation. How do we combine compassion with conviction, consciousness with practice? How do we encourage girls to recognize and resist sexism and other intersections of oppression in their lives? While girls and women still live, play, and work in a patriarchal playground, there are new realities for girls that did not exist for our feminist foremothers and foresisters. Today, environmental degradation, date rape drugs, the internet, and neo-conservatism are some of the social and political phenomena girls contend with. It may not be our role to "enlighten" girls to such phenomena; rather, it could be our role to mentor their own activism and advocacy that falls outside of consumerism. Too often, girls are overlooked for their unique and creative views on the world. An example of this would be our work with girls diagnosed and hospitalized for eating disorders. Practitioners cannot understand or fully appreciate the narratives of girls struggling with such a diagnosis without examining the context in which they are embedded. Even our psychological language is a barrier to comprehending the subjective narratives of girls. For example, Cushman (1995) says,

> The major implication of the empty self is that the empty self dovetails strikingly with the needs of the current economical and political system [and eerily, still does]. Psychotherapy theory not only reflects but also adds to the construction of the empty self. The empty self has both been "given" to us and is reproduced by us through our discourse and practices. Psychotherapy is thus in the position of contributing to the very ills it is attempting to heal. (p. 54)

As such, if we make an effort to recognize our own participation in the construction of pathology, we need also recognize how girls understand identities that are largely constitutive of such pathology. For girls with eating disorders, this means that their own contributions are often denied because the *Diagnostic and Statistical Manual of Mental Disorders* (4th ed.) (DMS-IV) (1994) constructs what it means to be an anorexic girl: "individuals with anorexia nervosa frequently lack insight into, or have considerable denial of, the problem and may be unreliable historians" (p. 540). Hence, our very human service canons reflect a bold juxtaposition against our experience consulting with girls.

White (2003) points out that we also disenfranchise clients by bringing the language of the marketplace into the therapy room. We discuss point systems, demerits, debits, credits, personal inventories, and so forth. If we claim to work with girls outside the narrow consumer construct, then we must implore ourselves to create a language that is indicative of the sensitive insights girls have, regardless of their DSM-IV label and moves beyond seeing them as psychological "consumers."

CO-CONSTRUCTING DIALOGUES

Discussing gender with girls, or associated gendered narratives, is not a monologue. Rather, we are co-constructing understanding and the personal meanings attached to identities deemed superficial by society (i.e. "adolescent," "girl," "anorexic"). Part of the challenge of co-construction, however, lies in the fact that practitioners may hear things we were not expecting, especially in regard to gender. Essentially, girls speak a different dialect and, as Bellafante (1998) ruefully acknowledges: "It's not surprising that Old Guard feminists, surveying their legacy, are dismayed by what they see" (p. 54).

This dismal view may be indicative of so-called second wave feminists ignoring the enormous spectrum of what girls/women/feminists can embody. At the same time, Bailey (1997) reminds us, "It may be incorrect and inefficient to believe or to foster the perception that the journey being embarked upon is an *essentially* new one. Valuable resources may be lost by assuming that current problems and concerns have no historical precedents" (p. 23, emphasis in original).

So we still must acknowledge that we endure sexism and until we can confidently assure girls we do not, we best listen to their interpretations of embodying gender. We must also acknowledge that the stories we elicit may be painful and carry the theme of violence and abuse we have fought so hard to end. Stories that ask us why we bothered if this gendered violence still endures?

And yet there is incredible hope in working with girls, especially in the sense that "A lesson we might take from this, however, is one expressed eloquently by many younger feminists: to learn to live more comfortably with ambiguity and contradiction" (Bailey, 1997, p. 17).

This is not so easy for those of us trained to identify labels and work with binaries: you are either "sick" or "well," "functional" or "dysfunctional," and this is further complicated for those of us who work with increasingly bigger case loads with less resources. We often do not have time for sitting with the ambiguity when our programs demand quantifiable outcomes.

Most importantly, this reality of contradiction often demands that we examine the contradiction in our own lives, as women and practitioners, and this can be less than comfortable. For example, many of us assume that second wave feminism "took care of things" and, because of this perspective, we are not vigilant to issues of sexism as they unfold in the lives of girls or in our workplaces. We especially enjoy Neuborne's (1995) reflections: "It's amazing what you can see when you are not hiding behind the warm, fuzzy glow of past feminist victories. It does not make me popular in the office. It does not even make me popular with women. Plenty of my female colleagues would prefer I quit rocking the boat" (p. 34).

She reminds us that just as girls are creating feminism differently, we are also addressing sexism differently. Our challenge to readers, however, is if "differently" means disguised as empty politically correct rhetoric, or worse, not at all.

CONCLUSION

We wish we could present a formula for practice that was simple and concrete (practitioner + skills + gender × sexism = social consciousness + change). As "our" girls constantly remind us, however, formulistic thinking leads to diluting the rich narratives of girls. Once diluted, they fit nicely with DSM-IV categories and take out any ambiguity to wrestle with. Such diluting also erases, at least to the practitioner's eyes, the nuances that intersect to create a girl's identity. Yet, as we have discussed, theorizing and categorizing do not render the narratives neutral. In fact, we believe that due to the embodied nature of gender, we are letting girls down by only reading off the surface of pathological diagnosis or presenting issue. We all concur that we want the best for girls, but how do we co-determine what constitutes "best" when girls have told us that female roles are limited? We know that we want girls to be safe, be happy, be strong and be successful, but have we stopped to reflect on what these actually mean? Have we stopped to consult with girls to unearth their aims, ambitions, challenges, and frustrations? And even with the best intentions, how have we condoned or perpetrated sexist and gendered ways of being with the very girls we aim to serve as practitioners? We have explored only a tiny territory on this vast and complex map named gender. We invite readers to take up new and creative means for examining how gender plays itself out in the lives of the girls we are so privileged to work with. Together, we can achieve a world that will no longer condone gendered violence of any form and co-construct the space needed for all people to develop their potential selves and contexts.

NOTES

1. By critical we mean that reflection is not a neutral exercise. The concept of reflection from our perspective requires substantial problematizing and positioning within the larger discourses and systems where such reflection occurs. Critical does not mean oppositional, rather it is a reminder to acknowledge, in our theorizing, inequities that exist due to race, gender, socio-economic status and sexual orientation.

2. The LIGIA Project (Listening to Girls' Interpretations of Adolescence) is funded by the Social Science and Humanities Research Council of Canada (SSHRC). Queries regarding the study should be addressed to the principal investigator, Dr. Marie Hoskins, at *mhoskins@uvic.ca*

3. We use the term consultants instead of participants to emphasize the importance of focusing on constructions of reality, experienced and described by the adolescent girls. By using this term in our focus group meetings at the very beginning of the project, it signaled to the girls that we took seriously the expert knowledge they had gained while in treatment for disordered eating.

4. Human service training programs generally include, child and youth care, social work, counselling and nursing.

5. see, for example, Adkins, 2001; Alexander, 1999; Arquette & Horton, 2000; Becker, Burwell, Gilman, Herzog, & Hamburg, 2002; Brown, 2002; Chaudhuri, 2001; Currie, 1997; Dunkley, Wertheim, & Paxton, 2001; Gornick, 1997; Harrison, 2000; Harrison & Cantor, 1997; Horton & Arquette, 2000; Krassas, Blauwkamp, & Wesselink, 2001; Mazzarella & Odom Pecora, 1999; McCabe & Ricciardelli, 2001; Milkie, 1999; Quart, 2003; Stice, Spangler & Agras, 2001; Strasburger, 2002; Turner & Hamilton, 1997; Vartanian, Giant, & Passino, 2001; Waller, Shaw, Hamilton, Baldwin, Harding & Summer, 1994; Wolf, 1991; Zavoina, 1999.

REFERENCES

Adkins, L. (2001). Cultural feminization: "Money, sex and power" for women. *Signs: Journal of Women in Culture and Society, 26,* 669-695.

Alexander, S. (1999). The gender role paradox in youth culture: An analysis of women in music videos. *Michigan Sociological Review, 13,* 46-64.

American Psychiatric Association. (1994). *Diagnostic and statistical manual of mental disorders* (4th ed.). Washington, DC: Author.

Arquette, C., & Horton, J. (2000, April). The influence of current television program-ming on the maintenance of female gender identity. Paper presented at the Annual Meeting of the American Educational Research Association (AERA), New Or-leans, LA.

Artz, S. (1997). On becoming an object. *Journal of Child and Youth Care, 11*(2), 17-37.

Bailey, C. (1997). Making waves and drawing lines: The politics of defining vicissi-tudes of feminism. *Hypatia, 12*(3), 17-28.

Becker, A. E., Burwell, R. A., Gilman, S. E., Herzog, D. B., & Hamburg, P. (2002). Eating behaviours and attitudes following prolonged exposure to television among ethnic Fijian adolescent girls. *British Journal of Psychiatry, 180*, 509-514.

Bell, S. (1993). Kate Bornstein: A transgender transsexual postmodern tiresias. In A. Kroker, & M. Kroker (Eds.), *The last sex: Feminism and outlaw bodies* (pp. 104-120). Montreal, Quebec: New World Perspectives.

Bellafante, G. (1998). Feminism: It's all about me! *Time, 151*, 48-54.

Brown, J. D. (2002). The mass media and American adolescent's health. *Journal of Adolescent Health, 31*,153-170.

Chaudhuri, M. (2001). Gender and advertisements: The rhetoric of globalization. *Women's Studies International Forum, 24*, 373-385.

Currie, D. H. (1994). "Going green": Mythologies of consumption in adolescent mag-azines. *Youth and Society, 26*, 92-117.

Currie, D. H. (1997). Decoding femininity: Advertisments and their teenage readers. *Gender and Society, 11*, 92-117.

Currie, D. H. (1999). *Girl talk: Adolescent magazines and their readers.* Toronto, ON: University of Toronto Press.

Currie, D. H. (2001). Dear Abby: Advice pages as a site for the operation of power. *Feminist Theory, 2*(3), 259-281.

Cushman, P. (1995). Psychotherapy in 1992. In D.K. Freedheim (Ed.), *History of psy-chology* (pp. 21-64). American Psychological Association.

Doza, C. (1995). Bloodlove. In B. Findlen (Ed.), *Listen up: Voices from the next femi-nist generation* (pp. 249-257). Seattle, WA: Seal Press.

Driscoll, C. (1999). Girl culture, revenge and global capitalism: Cybergirls, riot grrls, spice girls. *Australian Feminist Studies, 14*(29), 173-193.

Dunkley, T. L., Wertheim, E. H., & Paxton, S. J. (2001). Examination of models of multiple sociocultural influences on adolescent girls' body dissatisfaction and di-etary restraint. *Adolescence, 36*, 265-279.

Gergen, M. (2001). *Feminist reconstructions in psychology: Narrative, gender and performance.* Thousand Oaks, CA: Sage Publications.

Gornick, M. (1997). Reading selves, re-fashioning identity: Teen magazines and their readers. *Curriculum Studies, 5*(1), 69-86.

Harrison, K. (2000). The body electric: Thin-ideal media and eating disorders in ado-lescents. *Journal of Communication, 50*(3), 119-144.

Harrison, K., & Cantor, J. (1997). The relationship between media consumption and eating disorders. *Journal of Communication, 47*(1), 40-68.

hooks, b. (2000). *Feminist theory: From margin to center* (2nd ed.). Cambridge, MA: South End Press.

Horton, J., & Arquette, C. (2000, April). The role of television programming on secondary student's self identity. Paper presented at the Annual Meeting of the American Educational Research Association (AERA), New Orleans, LA.

Hoskins, M. L. (1997). *Difficulties with discourse: A metaphorical reading of reconstituting self.* Unpublished doctoral dissertation, University of Victoria, Victoria, British Columbia, Canada.

Krassas, N. R., Blauwkamp, J. M., & Wesselink, P. (2001). Boxing Helena and corseting Eunice: Sexual rhetoric in Cosmopolitan and Playboy magazines. *Sex Roles, 44*, 751-771.

Mazzarella, S. R., & Odom Pecora, N. (Eds.). (1999). *Growing up girls: Popular culture and the construction of identity* (Vol. 9). New York: Peter Lang Publishing.

McCabe, M. P., & Ricciardelli, L. A. (2001). Parent, peer, and media influences on body image and strategies to both increase and decrease body size among adolescent boys and girls. *Adolescence, 36*, 225-240.

McLuhan, M. (1964). *Understanding media: The extensions of man.* Cambridge, MA: MIT Press.

Mensinger, J. (2001). Conflicting gender roles prescriptions and disordered eating in single-sex and coeducational school environments. *Gender and Education, 13*(4), 417-429.

Milkie, M. A. (1999). Social comparisons, reflected appraisals and mass media: The impact of pervasive beauty images on black and white girls' self-concepts. *Social Psychology Quarterly, 62*, 190-210.

Nayer, D., & Chadha, G. (Producers), & Chadha, G. (Director). (2003). *Bend it like Beckham* [Motion Picture]. United States: Twentieth Century Fox Home Entertainment.

Neuborne, E. (1995). Imagine my surprise. In B. Findland (Ed.), *Listen up-voices from the next feminist generation* (pp. 29-35). Seattle, WA: Seal Press.

O'Brien Hallstein, D. L. (1999). A postmodern caring: Feminist standpoint theories, revisioned caring, and communications ethics. *Western Journal of Communication, 63*(1), 32-56.

Quart, A. (2003). *Branded: The buying and seeing of teenagers.* Cambridge, MA: Perseus Publishing.

Steinberg, L. (2002). *Adolescence* (6th ed.). New York: McGraw-Hill.

Stice, E., Spangler, D., & Agras, W. S. (2001). Exposure to media-portrayed thin-ideal images adversely affects vulnerable girls: A longitudinal experiment. *Journal of Social and Clinical Psychology, 20*, 270-288.

Strasburger, V. C., & Wilson, B. J. (Ed.). (2002). *Children, adolescents, and the media.* Thousand Oaks, CA: Sage Publications.

Thompson, D. (Ed.). (1995). *The Concise Oxford Dictionary* (9th Ed.). Oxford: Clarendon Press.

Turner, S. L., & Hamilton, H. (1997). The influence of fashion magazines on the body image satisfaction of college women: An exploratory analysis. *Adolescence, 32*, 603-614.

Vartanian, L. R., Giant, C. L., & Passino, R. M. (2001). "Ally McBeal vs. Arnold Schwarzenegger": Comparing mass media, interpersonal feedback and gender as predictors of satisfaction with body thinness and muscularity. *Social Behavior and Personality, 29,* 711-724.

Wald, G. (1998). Just a girl? Rock music, feminism and the cultural construction of female youth. *Signs: Journal of Women in Culture and Society, 23,* 585-610.

Waller, G., Shaw, J., Hamilton, K., Baldwin, G., Harding, T., & Summer, A. (1994). Beauty is in the eye of the beholder: Media influences on the psychopathology of eating problems. *Appetite, 23,* 287.

White, M. (2003). *Delight and the unexpected: Narrative therapy with individuals, families, groups and communities.* Conference, March, Vancouver, British Columbia, Canada.

Wolfe, N. (1991). *The beauty myth: How images of beauty are used against women.* Toronto, ON: Vintage Books/Random House.

Zavoina, S. C., & Carstarphen, M. G. (Eds.). (1999). *Sexual rhetoric: Media perspectives on sexuality, gender, and identity.* Westport, CT: Greenwood Press.

Using Popular Theatre for Engaging Racialized Minority Girls in Exploring Questions of Identity and Belonging

Jo-Anne Lee

Sandrina De Finney

SUMMARY. This chapter examines the use of popular theatre as a methodology to investigate racialized minority girls' processes of identity formation and experiences of exclusion and belonging in predominantly white, urban Victoria, B.C., Canada. The article draws on transnational feminist frameworks that emphasize intersectionality and locality to understand girls' processes of identity formation, cultural knowledges of exclusion and racialization, and practices and discourses of resistance. The article offers suggestions to assist practitioners, researchers, and policy-makers who wish to engage with expressive and theatre-based methods. *[Article copies available for a fee from The Haworth Document Delivery Service: 1-800-HAWORTH. E-mail address: <docdelivery@haworthpress.com> Website: <http://www.HaworthPress.com> © 2004 by The Haworth Press, Inc. All rights reserved.]*

Jo-Anne Lee, PhD, is Assistant Professor, Department of Women's Studies, Faculty of Humanities, University of Victoria. Sandrina De Finney, PhD candidate, is Assistant Professor, School of Child and Youth Care, Faculty of Human and Social Developmen, University of Victoria.

Address correspondence to: Dr. Jo-Anne Lee, Assistant Professor, Department of Women's Studies, Faculty of Humanities, University of Victoria, Victoria, BC, V8W 2Y2, Canada (E-mail: jalee@uvic.ca).

[Haworth co-indexing entry note]: "Using Popular Theatre for Engaging Racialized Minority Girls in Exploring Questions of Identity and Belonging." Lee, Jo-Anne, and Sandrina De Finney. Co-published simultaneously in *Child & Youth Services* (The Haworth Press, Inc.) Vol. 26, No. 2, 2004, pp. 95-118; and: *Working Relationally with Girls: Complex Lives/Complex Identities* (eds: Marie L. Hoskins, and Sibylle Artz) The Haworth Press, Inc., 2004, pp. 95-118. Single or multiple copies of this article are available for a fee from The Haworth Document Delivery Service [1-800-HAWORTH, 9:00 a.m. - 5:00 p.m. (EST). E-mail address: docdelivery@haworthpress.com].

Available online at http://www.haworthpress.com/web/CYS
© 2004 by The Haworth Press, Inc. All rights reserved.
Digital Object Identifier: 10.1300/J024v26n02_06

KEYWORDS. Intersectionality, identity development, popular theatre, transnational feminism, youthwork, youth work, critical pedagogy

This project was so awesome, I never thought I would get so much out of it. I always felt like I was so different living here, it's like you're from another planet or something, the way people look at you if you don't look like you belong here. I mean, I am always asked to explain myself or to explain my culture, why do I look this way, where am I from, all of that. And then we did the theatre project, and we talked about what that pressure is like for girls living here, what we go through every day, and we shared what it's like, and how we feel proud of who we are too, so we became like role models for other girls like us who feel like freaks because we could say we did something about it! (Taisha, 16)

Here we share some of the processes involved in using popular theatre (PT) as a research methodology for engaging girls from racialized ethnic minority backgrounds in research, and we critically reflect on our experiences. We found popular theatre to be a particularly rich and effective method to use in examining and making visible girls' experiences of identity formation.[1] As an interactive, expressive methodology, popular theatre helped girls in the study address issues of identity, silencing, and belonging in Victoria, BC, a predominantly white, mid-sized, Canadian city whose demographic and cultural origins are primarily British and European.

This chapter contributes to a growing body of research investigating the experiences of racialized minority youth who grow up in mainly white communities in Canada and elsewhere (Chalmers, 1997; Connolly, 2000; Fine, Stewart, & Zucker, 2000; Kakembo, 1994; Kaomea, 2003; Kelly, 1998; Lee, 2004; in press; Poteet, 2001; Varma-Joshi, Baker, & Tanaka, 2004).[2] The expressive and transformational nature of popular theatre was particularly well suited for involving young people in developing critical consciousness about their marginalization and working collaboratively to develop concrete strategies for social change (Anderson, Silverberg, & Michol, 1994; Cloutier, 1997; Fatkin, 1989; Holderness, 1992; Howarth, 1994; Lam, Ho, & Porter, 2002). It helped to engage and represent racialized girls' experiences in a form that respected their complex voices and realities.

POPULAR THEATRE AS A RESEARCH METHOD

Our approach to popular theatre was unique to our specific context. Although based on Theatre of the Oppressed (TO) techniques developed by Augusto Boal, a Brazilian activist, dramatist, and popular educator (Boal, 1979, 1992; Butterwick & Selman, 2003; Ferrand, 1995), the form of popular theatre we developed also borrowed from other popular theatre traditions from around the world,[3] incorporated suggestions from participants themselves, and was adapted to meet the particular needs of our setting and research questions. Our form of popular theatre also included other creative and participatory tools such as journaling, art, photo-narration, and a website.

Although the larger participatory action research project[4] pursued many questions, the specific questions explored through popular theatre included:

1. What is it like to be a racialized[5] girl growing up and living in a predominantly white urban center like Victoria?
2. What does growing up under a dominant culture of "whiteness"[6] mean for girls' sense of self and belonging?
3. How do we work with girls in ways that seriously consider the complexities of their lives, amplify their voices, and support them in taking action and becoming engaged with their communities?

The research incorporated transnational feminist frameworks to make sense of what we were hearing and seeing. Transnational feminist theories analyze issues of locality, migration, citizenship, nation, and mobility across borders and boundaries as they affect women and girls.[7] From this perspective, girls' multiple identities are seen as shaped by contextually specific intersecting cultural and social forces of race, ethnicity, class, gender, religion, sexualities, and globalization, among others.[8] These approaches are particularly relevant for addressing the experiences of racialized minority girls because they challenge homogenizing and universalizing conceptualizations of girls' identities and social locations.

Instead, transnational feminist approaches posit that place or locality play a significant role in mediating identity formation and girls' knowledge of self and culture (Lee, 2004; Lee, in press). Girls from racialized and immigrant minority backgrounds growing up in a context of dominant whiteness may have particular struggles and cultural knowledge around negotiating identity categories. In Victoria, where racialized girls are often invisible or made invisible, racialized girls' ability to speak about their lived realities may often be subsumed, silenced, and erased. Nonetheless, despite their inability to name their realities in public, girls still possess critical self-knowledge and insights into their lived realities. Such knowledge can potentially contribute to the theoretical landscape around identity formation and reshape research, practice and policy.

In this regard, Brown and Gilligan (1992) acknowledge the importance of relational aspects of work with girls and suggest participatory and expressive methodological processes that have built in the space for a girl to speak in her own voice and thus refuse the established story of a white, middle–class heterosexual woman's life, a story all girls in this culture–whether they are white or of color, rich or poor, heterosexual or lesbian–struggle against, albeit in different ways.

Prisha, 17, a participant in the popular theatre process, speaks to the systematic silencing or invisibility of her Muslim identity in Victoria and demonstrates critical self-knowledge about her reality.

> Okay, in Victoria, we're totally isolated; it's totally different from a bigger city like Vancouver. Here we have our own realities and our own issues because it's so white here! We never see many girls like us, like from our own backgrounds or our own religions. For me, I'm Muslim, and I never get to talk about that. It's so sad but it's true, it's totally not visible in my life here except with my family and like a few friends, but other than that I just always have to explain it if I want to talk about it and it's never just normal, you know? Like we always have to be educating the other girls, but I never just get to talk about being Muslim. It just feels like there are no places where we could go and talk about this stuff, just be ourselves without having to explain, but like even the school counselors don't understand, they just don't get it and it's so frustrating to go through life like that!

The systematic marginalization that Prisha and other research participants describe is also inherent to the research process. When undertaking community-based participatory action research with ethnic and racial minority girls in less cosmopolitan cities such as Victoria, suitable community-based organisations with whom to build research partnerships may not exist. In Victoria, there was only one community-based organisation that offered services to minority ethno-cultural youth and, in particular, girls. This led us to consider incorporating community development and popular theatre into a participatory action research project to mobilize community building and bring awareness to racialized girls' needs and experiences.

Although the use of popular theatre in research and practice with girls is relatively new, the field provides rich examples from across diverse communities for creating vehicles for transformative practice, critical consciousness, and social change (Anderson et al., 1994; Chamberlain, 1995; Salverson, 1996). Popular theatre, in its ability to mystify and un-settle, to create spontaneous creative spaces, to play, challenge, and symbolize, offered some distinct advantages over other methodologies for exploring notions of intersectionality, transnationalism, and pro-cesses of racialization in girls' lives. Through storytelling, dramatic in-terpretation, symbolic representations, and non-verbal and embodied techniques, popular theatre provides both a context and process for girls to safely try out different voices and positions, develop peer supports, and articulate their own cultural knowledges and emerging critical consciousness (Kondo, 1996).

PUTTING POPULAR THEATRE IN RESEARCH INTO PRACTICE

I suggested the name "It's About Us" [for the theatre project], be-cause girls need our own place to talk about girl stuff, our own ex-periences of what it's like, for me moving here from another country and all my daily life experience. Girls need places where we can help each other, meet other girls like us, support and teach each other and like let other girls know that they're not just alone going through that, we are too. (Taisha, 16)

Recruitment and Participation

To develop what the girls called "the theatre crew," we drew on a net-work of girls established through previous research and community connections and eventually formed a small group of ten girls (ages 14-18) from various backgrounds and experiences. About half of the girls had little if no experience with either theatre or with speaking in any formal ways about their experiences with issues like racism, cul-tural identity, gendered selves, and sexuality. We particularly sought girls willing and able to critically reflect on their experiences and who were interested in using the project as an avenue to explore their identities and social interactions. A few of the girls had been participants in a community theatre program for anti-racism education and had done extensive work around public speaking, facilitating workshops and presentations to audiences from the local community and across British Columbia. Some of the girls had previously participated in front-line youth programs at our partner agency, and some of those practice-based relationships were long-lasting and involved professional and personal relationships with the girls' families. It would have been almost impossible to begin a project of this magnitude and scope had we not already established relationships with the girls and their families through our community networks. Without these, we would have had to implement a more extensive process for relationship building with the individual girls, their families, and relevant networks and communities.[9]

Characteristics of Participants

It was important that the girls be somewhat open to community development and social action because they would be actors in public performances and involved as peer mentors and community leaders.

A participant expressed her willingness to be a leader in these terms:

> We want to do this work so we can let other girls like us know that they're not alone and sort of show how you can talk about these issues and that you can create change in your community. We don't want racialized girls to think they're all alone or for, like, teachers and youth counselors to ignore the issues just because they don't want to talk about racism or stuff like that. So we want to put this information out there to say, "yes, it's happening, and this is what you can do about it." (Taisha, 16)

Furthermore, despite the multiplicity of personal experiences and speaking locations, it was clear that the girls shared a common desire to become engaged in fuller conversations about themselves and this was at the crux of their willingness to become more engaged in taking action through popular theatre:

> Some things I have liked about this project were getting to know other girls like me, so I feel normal and I'm not the only one feeling confusion about my culture or about racism and stuff like that. It's good to talk about it with others who understand what you've been through. (Evelyn, 14)

I was really interested in this project because we've been talking about doing something just for girls like this for a long time, just starting something just for girls like us where we can share our experiences and support each other. (Taisha, 16)

I thought it would be a great opportunity to do something positive around the issues like racism and the stereotypes that people have about us. To help develop understanding in the community about who we are, to reach out to other girls like us who are isolated and who don't think anybody would understand their situation. (Manjeet, 16)

I decided to do this project because I am proud of being Chinese and that will never change, so I wanted to make friends who understand who I am and to learn new things to help me in the future in my career choice. (Barbara, 16)

Storytelling Lives Through Popular Theatre

During the first months of the project the girls worked with the Boal-trained Director of *Puente Theatre*, a well-established local theatre company, who had worked for years with immigrant and refugee women. We began with all-day group building workshops that combined program and research tasks (developing ethics and performance contracts, group process guidelines, group building, and scheduling) with theatre training. Our intention was to immediately create a space for dramatic play and exploration where the girls could begin to name, if even only through bodily gestures, daily experiences related to their racial, ethnic, gender and class identities. In keeping with Boal's techniques for Theatre of the Oppressed (TO), we incorporated theatre games and exercises into every step of the process to delve deeper into the stories, memories, and experiences that the girls shared. Each session consisted of a check-in circle while sharing snacks and drinks, warm-ups and cool downs, games and exercises, improvisations, and short vignettes. As the following quotes show, the girls enjoyed the embodied nature of theatre.

I really liked learning how to act, how to develop stories, how to project my voice and work with the other actors as a team, to use my body in a way that does something good. (Evelyn, 14)

> I gained a lot of confidence from doing the theatre, I feel like now I can speak about these issues without feeling shy or embarrassed that I will say the wrong thing, I feel so much more confident! (Manjeet, 17)

Rather than simply imposing the methods *onto* the girls and expecting them to fit into a preformed, aesthetically pure dramatic process, the activities first had to have meaning for the girls and be responsive to their realities, interests, and energy levels. Drawing on early lessons, we focused on popular theatre less as a prescriptive set of techniques and more on its ability to help develop playful interaction, nurture trust and relationships, and negotiate the sharing of stories and experiences. The process was deliberately left fluid and open-ended to allow the group to find its own identity and voice around the broad project themes. A range of TO methods such as working alone, in pairs, or in groups using poses, images, stories, improvisation, dynamization, and journaling were used to piece together pictures and stories based on themes such as home, feeling safe, not fitting in, "what I never tell anyone," and "strengths I have." In one exercise, when facilitators suggested the theme of "stereotypes people have about girls like me," the girls described their embodied experiences with racializing discourses and revealed the way racism and sexism intersect and play out in their lives.

> People think that because we're Asian females we're petite, we're not curvy, and we're "tight." (Evelyn, 14)

> They think because I'm Middle Eastern I'm all hairy and I have big hips. (Parshad, 17)

> Yeah, because I'm black they think I'll have this big booty and that I can dance, but then the guys don't really want to date black girls, they want the white girls who act black, so it's like "Well, where does that leave me?" (Taisha, 16)

Although women's different experiences of racialization and gendered racism have been described by other feminist authors and scholars,[10] what is significant about the girls' discussion is that by naming and sharing their experiences with peers, they created relational bonds that enabled them to explore sometimes submerged or silenced aspects of their identities. In becoming actors, they were able to reveal their own culturally derived consciousness about gendered, racialized, classed, and sexualized stereotypes. For example, initially some participants accepted and assumed the tourist rhetoric of Victoria as Canada's Little England and could not imagine that other girls like themselves also lived in the city and struggled with similar issues of living on the margins of whiteness.

> When they said there would be this project for girls like us, I was like, "Wow, there's other girls like me? Is anyone gonna show up?" I didn't think there would be, because I know who everyone is where I live and we all know who the other Muslim girls are, I was surprised to meet other Muslim girls I didn't know, it was so cool. (Parshad, 17)

Popular theatre nourished critical self-reflection, relationship building, peer support, and community building, hallmarks of effective participatory, feminist-based and action-oriented research and practice (Naples, 2003; Wolf, 1999).

The Final Product

Throughout the project, the girls also interviewed, photographed and videotaped themselves and their friends and met on their own to share and discuss their findings. Using theatre improvisation techniques, a series of skits emerged which resulted in a 1-hour dramatic presentation. During 5 months of almost weekly sessions, the girls developed a 1-hour production of three skits that were fleshed out and refined in preparation for a series of public performances, mainly to other racialized minority girls like themselves. Participants developed the characters, plots, and storylines and wrote the titles, scripts, and introductions to each skit. One of the skits, *Popularity*, became a forum theatre piece, meaning that audience members were invited to come on stage and engage with the actors to find solutions to the dilemmas posed in the skit. To give a sense of what our popular theatre work produced we provide the introductions, written by participants, and a short excerpt from each skit below.

A Day in the Life

> The first skit we are going to do is called *A Day in the Life*. It's about a girl's day in Victoria from the moment she wakes up in the morning. We want to show all the different parts of her life, all the

different messages she gets from different people who all contradict each other, like her friends, teachers, and neighbors. It shows how sometimes people judge you lower because they think you can't do something because they have an image of you. Maybe they got it from television, like how some people always assume that I used to live in a hut because I grew up in Ethiopia. Or they want you to be someone you're not, because they have a stereotype about who you are supposed to be. So the skit is about what it's like to deal with all those different messages from different people. (Taisha, 16)

Excerpt from A Day in the Life

Girl to teacher: I was just wondering why I got a low mark on my current events paper.

Teacher to girl: Well, racism is not really a current event, I mean you were supposed to write about something in the news that week, like the hydro dispute, or housing issues, or crime.

Girl to teacher: But racism *is* a current event, it happens all the time, it happens in our school every day, I mean it's a part of our lives.

Teacher to girl: I understand it affects your life, but the assignment was about a current issue that affects the whole province, something that has been in the news.

Curry Rice

This skit is called *Curry Rice*, it's about some of the dynamics that girls play out in school, it shows two groups of Asian girls who have a confrontation after class; the class is really boring, because the curriculum only talks about European history, so two of the girls, Chinese-Canadian girls, walk out yawning and bump into two Punjabi girls. They start insulting each other with all these racial stereotypes. This was our way of talking about everything we always think about other groups, but we never say it out loud, but it happens all the time between girls. This is how we judge who we hang out with and how we look and talk to other groups. (Janice, 16)

Excerpt from Curry Rice

> Girl 1: Bitch, why are you so upset, did your fancy Honda break down?
>
> Girl 2: What about you? Maybe your uncle forgot to pick you up in his taxi.
>
> Girl 1: Whatever, fried rice, are you pissed 'cuz you're so *short*?
>
> Girl 3: How would you know, I can't even tell you apart. Hinder, Binder, Jinder, you all look the same to me.

Popularity

> The next skit we will do is called *Popularity*. It's about popularity and fitting in junior high, it's a story that happened to me. The skit shows how some girls get pressured to fit in based on their looks and their clothes and how much damage you can cause if you start to question your own looks or compare them to someone you'll never be. Sometimes, girls think that to fit in, you have to look a certain way, like be thin with a certain body type, and look like you have light hair and light skin. But the only thing is many of us will never look like that. So, we wanted to show how that works and how you can react to it. This skit has a section where we will get some audience members to take the actors' place and change the story. So, this skit is called *Popularity*. (Evelyn, 14)

Excerpt from Popularity

> Girl 1: Could we do something to her hair . . . it needs to have high-lights or something.
>
> Girl 2: Yeah, it's so *dark* . . . so flat . . . so *depressing!*
>
> Girl 1: You *definitely* need some blond highlights to make your hair look shiny, prettier . . . and what are we going to do about your cleavage? You're so flat! Guys like boobs!
>
> Girl 2: Girl, we need to stuff your bra!

Analysis and Discussion of Scripts

The above excerpts provide a glimpse into girls' self-reflexive and previously unspoken stories of compulsory racism, heterosexism, and classism in their daily interactions with peers and adults.

In the first skit, *A Day in the Life*, the storyline uncovers pervasive yet implicit racisms embedded in the educational system. The central character speaks to the barriers and resistance she confronts in naming her experiences of racialization and making racism visible. The skit is her commentary on the hidden daily messages that she receives that work to erode her self-esteem and self-knowledge and against which she consciously resists by articulating a more critical and systemic definition of racism.

In the second skit, *Curry Rice*, the girls describe their experiences with horizontal (group to group) and internalized racism. Name calling and taunting are everyday experiences and expressions of gendered and racialized violence. The girls not only internalize powerful images of white female sexuality in popular culture, but they also actively participate in regulating and reproducing them. The skit's dialogue demonstrates the complicated racisms/sexisms that challenge the dominant understanding of racism as being about only skin color and black and white dichotomies, thus ignoring classed, gendered, sexualized, and other historical racisms.

Popularity tells the story of the effect of media images and popular culture on the girls' lives. In their experience at school, both popularity and "Canadianess" remain largely coded as white, thin, blonde, and blue-eyed (Lee, in press). Whiteness is normalized and linked to beauty, attractiveness, normality, popularity, and belonging. As played out in the skit, minority girls actively participate in maintaining normative standards of beauty, popularity and belonging by helping to lighten their friend to make her look more popular and acceptable. However, their participation is not voluntary but a consequence of larger structural and systemic forces that operate silently to shape their sense of self. Usually hidden from view, the post-performance discussions help actors and viewers to acknowledge, name, and understand how they work.

As the short excerpted vignettes demonstrate, popular theatre is particularly helpful in highlighting the daily struggles and resistances that girls enact to navigate their daily experiences of gendered and sexualized racisms.

Performance and Audience Reception

According to the tenets of popular theatre, the performance of theatre skits before an audience of peers is a way of validating and making visible erased experiences (Butterwick & Selman, 2003; Chamberlain, 1995; Fatkin, 1989). The introduction of audiences is a critical transition in any theatre process; this is the time when the stories come full circle and are communicated publicly and, in turn, shaped by the continuous loop of audience feedback and actors' reactions. The presentation's dramatic quality is an important aspect of crafting compelling pieces that effectively honor voices and engage audiences of peers. We wanted to translate to audiences the process of transformation and consciousness-raising experienced by participants in the theatre workshops. We hoped the presentation of skits would resonate with other girls in the audience in an empowering way. If audiences of girls could engage with the skits, either by confirming that the images and words enacted on the stage were reflective of their lives or by contesting and challenging the images and exposing their partialities, we would have succeeded in amplifying silenced voices and illuminating distorted realities. When the girls performed the skit, *Popularity*, in front of an audience of their peers, not surprisingly given the pervasive and systemic nature of racism, sexism, heterosexism and classism, audience members' individual interventions failed to alleviate the problematic encounter. Although the audience could clearly see acts of oppression on stage, their interventions only succeeded in making matters worse, not better. Individual interventions varied: some walked away, some reasoned and negotiated with the girl who was remaking her unpopular friend, and some tried to use their personal power to make things better, but all ended up failing to ameliorate the feelings of the oppressed actor. In follow-up discussions, the girl actors were empowered to speak for themselves about the systemic nature of gendered racisms in Victoria. The following excerpts from the presentation evaluations highlight the profound impact that the performance had on audience members.

> I was so amazed to see those girls up there, it was so real what they talked about, it was like, "This is my life!" (audience member)

> I liked that we could go up with the actors and try to find some solutions. It was really hard but at the same time it just shows how life is, how this is like for us all the time, there's just no easy an-

swers and you need people around you who support you no matter what, because racism will always be around. (audience member)

The *Curry Rice* skit was so real, what they said to each other, we do hear that all the time between groups. But for us on the reserve, it would have gone so much beyond that; it would have turned into a real fight right away instead of just being words. It would never just stay at that level of words. (audience member)

USING AN INTERSECTIONALITY FRAMEWORK IN WORK WITH MARGINALIZED GIRLS

In assembling drama-based strategies that honor girls' specific cultural knowledges, an important practical point is that what is not said or not picked up by the group matters as much as what makes it into the theatre skits or images. It is important in developing skits not to assume that the first themes and stories to emerge are the most important, the most widespread and shared, or the most revealing. The girls and facilitators collectively discussed, analyzed, and reviewed stories before selecting some for further skit development. Sometimes different research and stories were combined into a single skit, and sometimes several skits were prepared, tested on audiences, then revised and refined based on feedback. This collaborative process of probing, expanding, and questioning through different types of languages, images, and rhetorical processes was important in coming to critical consciousness about lived experiences. The project provided space and time for the girls to speak back to each other and engage in peer-to-peer sharing through performances, forums, discussions, interviews, check-ins or alternative storylines. This was neither a straightforward nor easy process and deserves further elaboration.

For example, in developing the skit, *Curry Rice*, whose storyline centers heavily on gendered racisms, the girls initially enacted scenes with explicit physical racial bullying. However, during discussions the girls revealed that this sort of explicit physical bullying happened much less often than the racial jokes, name calling, threats, and taunts that they ended up portraying in the skit. We realized that the girls possessed a very narrow understanding of racism.

Since the girls understood racism as defined only as individualized acts of physical violence, hatred, or bigotry, they did not necessarily have the language to name their own contradictory experiences of racism that were more likely to arise out of shifting processes of marginalization and subordination. Furthermore, shifting racialized markers such as physical features, style of clothes, or cultural signifiers continued to mark their difference from the accepted white norm. Instead of describing their experiences as racism, the participants used languages of exclusion such as "feeling misunderstood," "being the only yellow or brown girl," "having no place to be normal," "having violence because I am colored," "being excluded from what a real Canadian is," "feeling angry or sad about my culture," "not normal," "not sexy," "not popular," or "just different than them." By dissecting these stories about their daily interactions, the girls began to understand racism not only as physical violence but also as the subtle and systemic silencing and erasing of their realities.

In group discussions, the participants began taking up metaphors of belonging and exclusion and using them to name and challenge their experiences of gendered racism. Drawing on their words, the facilitators introduced a broader and more complex definition of racism to help reveal the different, varied, historically specific, institutionalized, and structured aspects of racialization and racism as they have affected different racialized groups in Canada. This naming process offered participants a far more complex vocabulary and meaning system through which they could understand their everyday lives.

However, it is important to reemphasize that for the girls acting out the *Curry Rice* skit, name-calling and taunts were never just superficial or innocent (i.e., names will never hurt me). We could see that they experienced the pain of racial taunting as palpable and visceral. This came out in our debriefs but was also visible and audible in their tone of voice, body postures, hand and facial gestures, and the frequent self-care and checking in with each other as they acted out the scenes. These interactions revealed the implicit bodily knowledges that girls carry and their strategic and tactical acts of both hidden and visible resistance.

However, this did not mean that for some girls, racial name-calling never escalated into physical violence.

EVALUATING THE POPULAR THEATRE PROCESS

Images and representations are open to many interpretations, and viewing relationships that take place between audience and actors are also unpredictable and varied. On the one hand, between the girls on stage and some audience members there was a direct connection, because the skits were experienced as "real." For many viewers, the performance was a positive, validating experience. Yet the veracity of the stories was possible because the girls themselves were actors, and some audience members found it difficult to separate the girls as actors and not real people. In part, this inability to project an imagined self is a matter of theatrical experience and training, something the girls as amateur actors had not had time to fully develop. Moreover, the ambiguities in their performances and in viewing relationships might also be linked to the social context of dominant whiteness in Victoria, where minority girls are often isolated and there is little opportunity for minority girls to develop critical consciousness of their own marginalization or that of the actors. Audience reactions revealed that racialized girls in Victoria had not learned to perceive their self-identities in complicated ways, simply because they remain in the shadows and are isolated from one another. This reality underscores the importance of considering social location and context in understanding racialized girls' lives. The experiences of cosmopolitan, heterogeneous urban centers cannot simply be generalized to more homogenous, less ethnically and racially diverse cities.

The opportunity to share and validate hidden knowledge was a crucial aspect of the girls' ability to voice submerged consciousness about their "doubled selves" or multiple subjectivities.[11] Through dramatic play, many of the girls began to see themselves as reflected through the eyes of dominant, heterosexual, and middle class whiteness. Once they saw, named, and voiced this location, they were able to speak back to it as insiders to their outsider status (Nandy, 1989).

Developing peer relationships with others like themselves through the theatre project enabled the girls to see their doubled selves as socially constructed. One important finding in our experience with popular theatre as a research method is that racialized girls do possess the knowledge to name their realities and to speak against their marginalization when given the opportunity to share and reflect on their experiences. Even in their daily lives, it is clear that cultural knowledge is required for them to successfully negotiate signifiers of difference such as clothes, accent, physical characteristics, socio-economic status, and sexuality, among others. To successfully make their way through and across many cultural worlds, racialized minority girls require a broad spectrum of cultural knowledges that have yet to be recognized and validated. As researchers and practitioners, we often fail to recognize and acknowledge racialized girls' strategies for moving across and between the different cultural spheres of their everyday lives.

IMPLICATIONS FOR FACILITATORS, PRACTITIONERS, AND RESEARCHERS

One important insight around incorporating theatre-based approaches with girls and young people in general is that the methods are not inherently empowering and participatory; when applied purely as a dramatic tool, they can seem didactic and constraining (Seebaran & Johnston, 1998; Shepard, 1995). When the director attempted to replicate a specific technique, activity, or game in strict accordance with an acting method, the girls would quickly lose interest and would begin to resist by removing their energy and presence from the circle.

> With the facilitation, I think sometimes we wasted a lot of time doing the steps, the warm-up exercises when we already knew what we wanted to do, so I think we should have just jumped in right away, it was just like, "What's the point?" (Eva, 14)

Another important lesson garnered from the project is that when dealing with sensitive and invisible topics such as racism and sexism, facilitators must be prepared to dig deeper and assess what the stories—whether silenced, untold, contested, or enthusiastically taken up—say and reflect about participants' lived realities. Popular theatre facilitators need to foster critical consciousness by suggesting alternative interpretations and narratives for realities that remain unacknowledged or distorted by dominant discourses. They must provide space and alternative language to connect broader historical, economic, political, and sociocultural processes to personal narratives. They cannot be content to simply collect and perform stories and to leave interpretations up to participants and audiences. As are our own, girls' discourses and understanding of their own multiple locations are mediated by dominant discourses that need to be explicated and teased out through critical dialogue and other expressive means. Popular theatre proved an effective–if not always fully sufficient–discursive method to explore these realities.

To draw the links between the global and local, to validate the specificities of individual girls' lives, and to provide a context for interpretation, practitioners, policy-makers, and researchers must engage language and approaches that more fully map out, acknowledge, and effectively work with the complexities of racialized girls' lives without overgeneralizing and essentializing them through unreflexive use of cultural stereotypes. Popular theatre, when juxtaposed with transnational feminist analytical frameworks, offer powerful tools for uncovering and connecting interactions between the personal and the global.

To illustrate, when the girls described their experiences through notions of Otherness, they revealed complicated dynamics of belonging and exclusion. However, they experienced exclusion not only within the dominant culture and groups but also in relation to dominant norms within their own ethno-cultural communities. In more than one group session, discussions about ethnicity produced tensions. Some wanted to valorize their ethnic backgrounds as a defense against racism, while others rejected their difference to claim belongingness to the Canadian mainstream. Transnational feminist concepts of cultural hybridity, diasporic identities, and flexible citizenship allowed the girls to understand that their identity positions are continually emerging, historically, socially and culturally formed, and not fixed in their ethno-cultural heritage. Through these alternative explanations, they began to name the complex ways that power operates within and without ethnic minority and dominant majority cultural spheres.

CONCLUSION

Our approach to popular theatre as a research tool was rooted in a commitment to transparency and accountability. In writing collaboratively about this project, we gained more awareness about the contradictions and dilemmas inherent in what we hoped to achieve. Many important methodological dilemmas emerged that are beyond the scope of this chapter but that warrant deeper discussion and which we continue to address in other forums.

When methods of popular theatre, as other expressive approaches, are delivered without a critical lens and consistent evaluation, they can replicate problematic structures, processes, and representations that reessentialize and recolonize. Furthermore, the types of whole conversations we advocate can never be completely and unproblematically representative or wholly transparent and visible, as these are constantly shaped and negotiated relationally and contextually and bound by existing discourses and social structures. Even with these potential pitfalls, when undertaken reflexively popular theatre remains an alternative and promising research methodology. It is nonetheless a demanding, long-term, but personally involving and rewarding process for girls and facilitators.

NOTES

1. This popular theatre project was a component of a larger four-year community development/PAR project with over 100 girls and young women. Participatory Action Research (PAR) is a research framework that links research to social action and social change by including research participants in all aspects of the research process; see Freire, 1996; Hart, 1997; Messer-Davidow, 1991; Park, Brydon-Miller, Hall & Jackson, 1993; Salverson, 1996; Tandon, 2002.

2. Despite the nascent and limited body of research in Canada, researchers in Great Britain and the United States have undertaken comparable research (for example, Carrington & Short, 1993; Gilborn, 1996; Lewis, 2001; MacPhee, 1997; Troyna & Hatcher, 1992).

3. See Colleran & Spencer, 1998; Farrow, 1993; Schechter, 2003; Shutzman & Cohen-Cruz, 1994; Young & Barrett, 2001.

4. See P. Maguire, 1987 and R. McTaggart, 1997 for definitions and models.

5. According to Miles (1989), racialization refers to the dialectic process by which groups are categorized as different based on perceived cultural, physical, and social characteristics. These characteristics vary historically, though they are usually somatic features like skin color, but other non-biological and inferred characteristics have been used, such as religious markers, intelligence and performance measures, and supposed personality traits. Through racialization, certain groups such as white Euro-Canadians are racialized as normal, while other groups are racialized as "other," as outsiders, or as inferior. Although we acknowledge that the notion of race is not real, the *impact* and *effects* of race-based thinking and racial hierarchies are very real. The notion of racialization captures how and why certain racial characteristics are taken up by or imposed on differentiated groups, thus sustaining the stratification of social systems, structures and institutions.

6. For useful conceptualizations of whiteness as a social formation, see Dyer, 1997; Frankenberg, 1997; Perry, 2002; Rothenberg, 2002; and Winddance-Twine, 1996. Scholars of whiteness understand whiteness as more than a racial identity based on skin colour. Whiteness is a cultural system that is continuously changing and is ideologically, materially and historically based. As a dominant cultural system, Whiteness defines the 'center' and therefore also what is not normal, or what is 'other' than normal. Whiteness maintains its hegemony through dominant social formations such as political systems, the media, and educational institutions. We have chosen not to capitalize the term, 'whiteness' when referring to whiteness as a social and cultural formation and not a racial or biological identity to signal our naming of the specific hegemonic cultural contexts that racialized minority girls encounter in growing up in Victoria, BC.

7. Transnationalism focuses on the movements within, between, and across national borders. This conceptual framework helps us think about the borders and boundaries in racialized girls' lives and the ways that girls negotiate the crossing and bridging of their identity locations, whether consciously or unconsciously. Transnational feminists dispute the notion of one universal category of identity and instead look at contextual, historical and spatial specifics of identity formation, particularly the role of nationalism and state formation in identity formation. They further acknowledge that

forms of domination shift and move as subjects move across borders, as captured in Grewal & Kaplan's (1994) notion of scattered hegemonies. See also Brah, 1996; Frankenberg & Mani, 1996; Friedman, 1998; Narayan & Harding, 2000; Ong, 1999, Westwood & Phizaklea, 2000.

8. The field of youth studies has tended to be dominated by traditional psychological frameworks, that have not always illuminated the social and material contexts through which girls' social identities are shaped (Maguire, 2001; Morawski, 2001; Perry, 2002; Tolman & Brydon-Miller, 2001, 1997). Much of the research literature on adolescent girls or racial minority youth problematically construct identity categories such as gender, race, ethnicity, and citizenship as fixed, uni-dimensional, separate, and taken for granted. Moreover, rather than viewing these as provisional categories of identity that overlap and interact with each other, traditional research approaches have seen them as discrete units which researchers compare as categories (Beiser, Shik & Curyk, 2003; Bibby, 2001; Carlson, 2000; Giroux, 1993; Morawski, 2001). Furthermore, theories of child development and children's ecologies have tended to emphasize the experiences of white, middle-class, heterosexual boys, while other identities have fallen by default under the banners of diversity studies or cross-cultural psychology (Jackson, 1997; Robinson, 2005; Smith, 2004). And, while they describe the systems that shape children's identities and their impact on children's development, developmental and ecological theories do not necessarily reveal how social formations—for example, the family, educational systems, peer relations—are themselves shaped and sustained (Giroux, 1993; Perry, 2002; Robinson, 2005).

9. It is not unusual in PAR and community research involving young people, for researchers, resources and participants to become engaged along a continuum throughout the project, and for community capacity to become crystallized through a 'scaffolding' of participation and involvement. However, this sort of generative process is also embedded in problematic issues about girls' limited access to funding, status, power, and methods of knowledge production and dissemination. We consciously organized an advisory group of girls, agencies and policy-makers whose mandates or areas of concern dealt with issues affecting immigrant, refugee and established communities of color. These initiatives represent some of the community development aspects of the larger study that built a network and infrastructure to sustain the girls' actions and locate funding sources after the end of the research project.

10. See in particular Anzaldua, 2002; Bannerji, 2000; Jiwani, Janovicek & Cameron, 2001.

11. By 'doubled selves' we refer to Fanon's (1986) insight into the development of doubled consciousness through the process of racialization. We already described how racialization operates to create dominant and subordinate social categories. According to Fanon, the dominant group's denial of recognition of the Other forces the Other to see herself reflected through the deliberately distorted gaze of the dominant group. Yet, Fanon goes on to demonstrate that when the Other becomes conscious of this distortion, she gains a doubled or critical consciousness of self; her 'self' as Other contradicts her own knowledge of her 'self' as whole and as not split or distorted. The development of critical doubled consciousness may lead to passive, hidden and sometimes overt resistance to dominant or hegemonic discourses and oppressive practices.

REFERENCES

Anderson, J., Silverberg, J., & Michol, J. (1994). *Ready for action: A popular theatre popular education manual.* Waterloo Public Interest Research Group.

Anzaldúa, G. E. (2002). (Un)natural bridges, (un)safe spaces. In G. E. Anzaldúa & A. Keating, (Eds.), *This bridge we call home: Radical visions for transformation* (pp. 1-6). New York: Routledge.

Baker, R., Panter-Brick, C., & Todd, A. (1996). Methods used in research with street children in Nepal. *Childhood: 'Children out of place': Special issue on working and street children, 3 (2), 171-94.*

Bannerji, H. (2000). *The dark side of the nation: Essays on multiculturalism, nationalism and gender.* Toronto, ON: Canadian Scholar's Press.

Beiser, M. A., Shik, A., & Curyk, M. (2003). *New Canadian children and youth study literature review.* Retrieved June 11, 2003, from http://www.ceris.metropolis.net/Virtual%20Library/other/beiser1.html

Bibby, R. W. (2001). *Canada's teens: Today, yesterday and tomorrow.* Toronto, ON: Stoddart.

Boal, A. (1979). *Theatre of the oppressed* (C. A. McBride & M. L. McBride, Trans.). New York: Urizen Books (Original work published 1979).

Boal, A. (1992). *Games for actors and non-actors* (A. Jackson, Trans.). New York: Routledge. (Original work published 1992).

Brah, A. (1996). *Cartographies of diaspora: Contesting identities.* London: Routledge.

Brown, L. M., & Gilligan, C. (1992). *Meeting at the crossroads: Women's psychology and girls' development.* Cambridge, MA: Harvard University Press.

Butterwick, S., & Selman, J. (2003). Deep listening in a feminist popular theatre project: Upsetting the position of audience in participatory education. *Adult Education Quarterly, 54*(1), 7-22.

Carlson, C. (2000). Ethnic differences in processes contributing to the self-esteem of early adolescent girls. *Journal of Early Adolescence, 20*(1), 44-67.

Carrington, B., & Short, G. (1993). Probing children's prejudice: A consideration of the ethical and methodological issues raised by research and curriculum. *Educational Studies, 19,* 163-179.

Chalmers, V. (1997). White out: Multicultural performances in a progressive school. In M. Fine, L. Weis, L. Powell & L. M. Wong (Eds.), *Off white: Readings on race, power, and society* (pp. 66-78). New York: Routledge.

Chamberlain, F. (1995). *Contemporary theatre review: An international journal.* Malaysia: Harwood Academic Publishers.

Cloutier, J. L. (1997). *Popular theatre, education, and inner city youth.* Unpublished master's thesis, University of Alberta, Edmonton, Alberta, Canada.

Colleran, J. M., & Spencer, J. S. (1998). *Staging resistance: Essays on political theater.* Ann Arbor, MI: University of Michigan Press.

Connolly, P. (2000). Racism and young girls' peer-group relations: The experience of South Asian girls. *Sociology, 34*(3), 499-519.

Dyer, R. (1997). *White.* New York: Routledge.

Fanon, F. (1986). *Black skin, White masks.* London: Pluto Press.

Farrow, H. L. (1993). *Local organizing and popular theatre: Case studies from Namibia and South Africa.* National Library of Canada: Ottawa, ON.

Fatkin, G. Y. K. (1989). *Anti-racism themes in theatre for young audiences: Teaching tolerance through drama.* National Library of Canada: Ottawa, ON.

Ferrand, L. (1995). Forum theatre with carers: The use of forum theatre in specific community settings. In F. Chamberlain, (Ed.), *Contemporary theatre review: An international journal* (pp. 23-39). Malaysia: Harwood Academic Publishers.

Fine, M., Stewart, A. J., & Zucker, A. N. (2000). White girls and women in the contemporary United States: Supporting or subverting race and gender domination? In C. Squire (Ed.), *Culture in psychology* (pp. 59-72). London & Philadelphia: Routledge.

Frankenberg, R. (Ed.). (1997). *White displacing Whiteness: Essays in social and cultural criticism.* Durham: Duke University Press.

Frankenberg, R., & Mani, L. (1996). Crosscurrents, crosstalk: Race, 'postcoloniality,' and the politics of location. In S. Lavie & T. Swedenberg (Eds.), *Displacement, diaspora and geographies of identity* (pp. 273-294). London: Duke University Press.

Freire, P. (1996). *Pedagogy of the oppressed.* London: Penguin Books.

Friedman, S. S. (1998). *Mappings: Feminism and the cultural geographies of encounter.* Princeton: Princeton University Press.

Gillborn, D. (1996). Student roles and perspective in antiracist education: A crisis of White ethnicity? *British Educational Research Journal, 22,* 165-179.

Giroux, H. A. (1993). *Living dangerously: Multiculturalism and the politics of difference.* New York: Peter Lang Publishing.

Grewal, I., & Kaplan, C. (Eds.). (1994). *Scattered hegemonies: Postmodernity and transnational feminist practice.* Minneapolis, MN: University of Minnesota Press.

Hart, R. (1997). *Children's participation: The theory and practice of involving young citizens in community development and environmental care.* London: Earthscan.

Holderness, G. (1992). *The politics of theatre and drama.* London: MacMillan.

Howarth, C. M. (1994). *An examination of facilitation in three popular theatre projects with young adults.* Unpublished master's thesis, University of Alberta, Edmonton, Alberta, Canada.

Jackson, D. (Ed.). (1997). *Minorities and girls in school: Effects on achievement and performance.* Thousand Oaks, CA: Sage Publications.

Jiwani, Y., Janovièek, N., & Cameron, A. (2001). *Erased realities: The violence of racism in the lives of immigrant and refugee girls of colour.* Vancouver, BC: BC/Yukon FREDA Centre for Research on Violence Against Women & Children.

Kakembo, P. (1994). *BLAC report on education: Addressing inequalities–empowering Black learners.* Halifax, NS: BLAC.

Kaomea, J. (2003). Reading erasures and making the familiar strange: Defamiliarizing methods for research in formerly colonized and historically oppressed communities. *Educational Researcher, 32* (2), 14-25.

Kelly, J. (1998). *Under the gaze: Learning to be Black in White society.* Halifax, NS: Fernwood Publishing.

Kondo, D. (1996). The narrative production of 'home,' community, and political identity in Asian American theater. In S. Lavie & T. Swedenberg (Eds.), *Displacement, diasporas and geographies of identity* (pp. 97-117). London: Duke University Press.

Lam, A., Ho, C. Y., & Porter, V. R. (2002). *Games and stories: A guide to theatre for dialogue and community.* Jump Start Consulting and Training: Vancouver, BC.

Lee, J. (2004). Racialized minority and First Nations girls and young women in Victoria. *BC: Friends of Women & Children in B.C.: Report card on women and children in B.C, 3(5).* Retrieved October 21, 2004, from *http://www.wmst.ubc.ca/Reports.htm*

Lee, J. (in press). Canaries in a cage: Racialized girls living in, through, under and over whiteness: Issues of citizenship, identity and social cohesion on the edge of empire. In N. Angeles and P. Gurstein (Eds.), *Engaging civil societies in democratic planning and governance (Working Title).* Toronto, ON: University of Toronto Press.

Lewis, A. (2001). There is no 'race' in the schoolyard: Color-blind ideology in an (almost) all-White school. *American Educational Research Journal, 38,* 781-811.

MacPhee, J. (1997). That's not fair! A White teacher reports on White first graders' responses to multicultural literature. *Language Arts, 74,* 33-40.

Maguire, P. (2001). The congruency thing: Transforming psychological research and pedagogy. In D. Tolman & M. Brydon-Miller (Eds.), *From subjects to subjectivities: A handbook of interpretive and participatory methods* (pp. 276-290). New York: University Press.

Maguire, P. (1987). *Doing participatory research: A feminist approach.* Amherst, MA: Center for International Education, University of Massachusetts.

McTaggart, R. (Ed.). (1997). *Participatory action research: International contexts and consequences.* New York: State University of New York Press.

Messer-Davidow, E. (1991). Academic knowledge and social change: Know-how. In J. Hartman & E. Messer-Davidow (Eds.), *(En) gendering knowledge: Feminists in academe* (pp. 281-310). Knoxville, TN: University of Tennessee Press.

Miles, R. (1989). *Racism.* London: Routledge.

Morawski, J. (2001). Feminist research methods: Bringing culture to science. In D. Tolman & M. Brydon-Miller (Eds.), *From subjects to subjectivities: A handbook of interpretive and participatory methods* (pp. 57-76). New York: New York University Press.

Nandy, A. (1989). *The intimate enemy: Loss and recovery of self under colonialism.* Delhi: Oxford University Press.

Naples, N. (2003). *Feminism and method: Ethnography, discourse analysis, and activist research.* New York: Routledge.

Narayan, U., & Harding, S. (Eds.). (2000). Introduction. *Decentering the center: Philosophy for a multiculturalist, postcolonial, and feminist world* (pp. vii-xv). Indianapolis: Indiana University Press.

Ong, A. (1999). *Flexible citizenship: The cultural logics of transnationality.* Durham: Duke University Press.

Park, P., Brydon-Miller, M., Hall, B., & Jackson, T. (Eds.). (1993). *Voices of change: Participatory research in the United Stated and Canada.* Toronto, ON: OISE Press.

Perry, P. (2002). *Shades of white: White kids and racial identities in high school.* London: Duke University Press.

Piran, N. (2001). Re-inhabiting the body from the inside out: Girls transform their school environment. In D. Tolman & M. Brydon-Miller (Eds.), *From subjects to subjectivities: A handbook of interpretive and participatory methods* (pp. 218-239). New York: New York University Press.

Poteet, M. B. (2001). *Cultural identity and identity performance among Latin American youths in Toronto.* Unpublished master's thesis, York University, Toronto, Ontario, Canada.

Robinson, T. (2005). *The convergence of race, ethnicity and gender: Multiple identities in counseling.* Upper Saddle River, NJ: Pearson Merrill Prentice Hall.

Rothenberg, P. S. (Ed.). (2002). *White privilege: Essential readings on the other side of racism.* New York: Worth Publishers.

Salverson, J. (1996). *The unimaginable occurrence: Storytelling, popular theatre and an ethic of risk.* Unpublished master's thesis, University of Toronto, Toronto, Ontario, Canada.

Schecter, J. (Ed.). (2003). *Popular theatre: A sourcebook.* New York: Routledge.

Schutzman, M., & Cohen-Cruz, J. (Eds.). (1994). *Playing Boal: Theatre, therapy and activism.* London: Routledge.

Seebaran, R. B., & Johnston, S. P. (1998). *Anti-racism theatre projects for youth.* Ministry Responsible for Multiculturalism and Immigration, BC.

Shepard, K. E. (1995). *Get with the act! The impact of popular theatre on anti-racist education.* Unpublished master's thesis, University of Guelph, Guelph, Ontario, Canada.

Smith, T. B. (2004). *Practicing multiculturalism: Affirming diversity in counseling and psychology.* Boston, MA: Pearson Education Inc.

Tandon, R. (2002). *Participatory research: Revisiting the roots.* New Delhi: Mosaic Books.

Tolman, D., & Brydon-Miller, M. (1997). *Transforming psychology: interpretive and participatory research methods.* Malden, MA: Blackwell.

Tolman, D., & Brydon-Miller, M. (Eds.). (2001). *From subjects to subjectivities: A handbook of interpretive and participatory methods.* New York: New York University Press.

Troyna, B., & Hatcher, R. (1992). *Racism in children's lives: A study of mainly-White primary schools.* London: Routledge.

Tuhiwai-Smith, L. (1999). *Decolonizing methodologies: Research and indigenous peoples.* London: Zed Books.

Winddance-Twine, F. (1996). Brown skinned White girls: Class, culture and construction of white identity in suburban communities. *Gender, Place and Culture, 3* (2), 205-224.

Varma-Joshi, M., Baker, C. J., & Tanaka, C. (2004). Names will never hurt me. *Harvard Educational Review, 74*(2), 175-208.

Westwood, S., & Phizacklea, A. (2000). *Transnationalism and the politics of belonging.* London: Routledge.

Wandor, M. (1986). *Carry on understudies: Theatre and sexual politics.* London: Routledge & Kegan Paul.

Wolf, D. (Ed.). (1999). *Feminist dilemmas in fieldwork.* Boulder, CO: Westview Press.

Young, L., & Barrett, H. (2001). Issues of access and identity: Adapting research methods with Kampala street children. *Childhood, 8* (3), 383-395.

Radical Pragmatism: Prevention and Intervention with Girls in Conflict with the Law

Marge Reitsma-Street

SUMMARY. The article introduces radical pragmatism, an approach to working with girls in conflict with the law based on experience, research, and theory, including an analysis of the structural and gendered inequities in which girls live and make choices. There are three components. First, abolish punitive practices and stereotypes that do not attend to girls' requirements of well-being. Second, expand what does work, including the effective, efficient community and school programs that prevent crime and promote well-being as well as differential interventions and compensatory, restorative initiatives for individual girls and groups. Third, politicize the need for equity and human rights by listening to what girls say they require to heal the hurts and prevent additional ones and by ensuring parity in funds and programs that build on what girls require. *[Article copies available for a fee from The Haworth Document Delivery Service: 1-800-HAWORTH. E-mail address: <docdelivery@haworthpress.com> Website: <http://www.HaworthPress.com> © 2004 by The Haworth Press, Inc. All rights reserved.]*

Marge Reitsma-Street, PhD, is Professor, Studies in Policy Practice and School of Social Work, Faculty of Human and Social Development, University of Victoria.

Address correspondence to: Dr. Marge Reitsma-Street, Studies in Policy and Practice, Faculty of Human and Social Development, University of Victoria, Box 1700, Victoria, BC, V8W 2Y2, Canada (E-mail: mreitsma@uvic.ca).

The author appreciates the assistance of Sibylle Artz and Diana Nicholson in preparing this article.

[Haworth co-indexing entry note]: "Radical Pragmatism: Prevention and Intervention with Girls in Conflict with the Law." Reitsma-Street, Marge. Co-published simultaneously in *Child & Youth Services* (The Haworth Press, Inc.) Vol. 26, No. 2, 2004, pp. 119-137; and: *Working Relationally with Girls: Complex Lives/Complex Identities* (ed: Marie L. Hoskins, and Sibylle Artz) The Haworth Press, Inc., 2004, pp. 119-137. Single or multiple copies of this article are available for a fee from The Haworth Document Delivery Service [1-800-HAWORTH, 9:00 a.m. - 5:00 p.m. (EST). E-mail address: docdelivery@haworthpress.com].

Available online at http://www.haworthpress.com/web/CYS
© 2004 by The Haworth Press, Inc. All rights reserved.
Digital Object Identifier: 10.1300/J024v26n02_07

KEYWORDS. Girls and crime, abolition, differential intervention, human rights, juvenile offenders, juvenile justice

The purpose of this article is to present a radical and pragmatic way of working with girls who may or do break laws. The radical nature of the approach is rooted in an appreciation of the structural context in which laws, policies, discourses, and everyday practices are gendered and affect the choices girls have to make sense of their lives and to choose behaviors. The pragmatic essence of the approach is embedded in years of experience and research into the complex realities of girls' lives and their different pathways to delinquency. It is also rooted in an examination of what promotes the well-being of different girls under different conditions. The specific aspects of radical pragmatism are to abolish what does not work, expand what does, and politicize equity and human rights.

UNDERSTANDING CRIME AND GIRLS

Girls, like boys, break the law, but not as often. In historical and recent research, it is clear that girls in Canada and elsewhere commit serious crimes infrequently. Despite the public concern about an increase in girl crime and fears of female violence (Moretti, Odgers, & Jackson, 2004), only 4.9 percent of all Canadians charged by police in 2002 for breaking criminal laws are girls. Although girls engage in illegal behaviours, they rarely develop crime specialties (Chesney-Lind & Pasko, 2004; Reitsma-Street, 1999). On self-report surveys, the majority of girls report committing several illegal or destructive acts in the last year or two, with a small minority reporting more frequent misbehaviours (Artz, Riecken, MacIntyre, Lam, & Maczewski, 1999; Hagan & McCarthy, 1997; Marcus, 1999). In studies of youth health, for example, it is striking to read that few youth–boys or girls (approximately 3 percent in random samples)–report receiving injuries from fighting, but 41% report an injury in the past year from playing sports or household or transportation accidents (Browne, 2003).

Youth crime in Canada and the USA appears to have increased modestly as has the size of the youth population from the 1970s until the middle of the 1990s. But the statistics do not indicate an explosion of female crime (Chesney-Lind & Okamot, 2001). The absolute numbers of charges for both males and females increased after the 1984 introduction of the *Young Offenders Act* in most, but not all, Canadian provinces (Reitsma-Street, Artz, & Nicholson, in press). There are various reasons for the apparent increases in the USA and Canada. The upper age limit that defines youth in the youth justice system has changed over time, as has the definition of what constitutes a crime. Status offences have been decriminalized while administrative offences and non-compliance breaches have been added to the laws. The total population of youth also increased up to the mid-1990s in North America, and changes in charging patterns by school officials, police, and prosecutors pushed up crime rates (Carrington, 1999; Doob & Sprott, 1998; Estrada, 2001). Thus, the proportions of females charged by police per 100,000 female youth population started to decline late in the 1990s, and the comparable rate for boys dropped even more. The number of females charged by police was 2,230 per 100,000 Canadian female youth in 1996, 1,891 by 1999, and 2,046 by 2001 (Statistics Canada, 2002).

In the early 1980s, 1 in 10 cases charged with a crime and appearing in youth courts were against girls. Twenty years later the gender ratio narrowed to 1 in 5 as charge rates laid against girls increased more than rates for boys. This may mean males are offending less or officials are more often laying more charges against girls for particular offences, such as those against administrative of justice. In 1986, 6.1% of charges laid in Canadian youth court against girls were for administrative offenses such as not complying with a probation order, increasing to 20.9% in 1988 and rising steadily through the 1990s. By 2000, 33.8% of all charges were for these types of offenses, making them the most frequent charge laid against girls. Administrative charges for boys has also increased, but not so sharply.

Next in frequency for both sexes are charges for theft under $5000 and possession of stolen goods. Less frequent were charges for major crimes against property and minor ones against the public order and people, including possession of drugs. Infrequent, but all too problematic and horrific, are the charges for serious violent crimes against people. The low rate of violent charges compared to more prevalent administrative and theft charges is consistent over the years from 1992 to 2000. The most striking change is a decrease in theft charges and an increase in administrative ones. There is no clear trend over the past decade in the percent of charges for either minor or major assaults.

Girls who commit crimes do more than break laws. Their behaviors are actions that cross the boundaries of what is acceptable and good. These boundaries are constructed by powerful adults whether parents, teachers, journalists, counselors, or justice officials who decide through words, practices, policies, and criminal law the boundaries of what is legal and what is not, what is feminine or sexy and what is not, what is productive and important, and what is not valued in everyday life (Walkerdine, Lucey, & Melody, 2001). Girls themselves make decisions about what borders are important. They judge, often harshly, what is good or undesirable, and they police others in terms of reputation, attitude, and status (Williams, 2002).

But it is the adults and organizations who have more power and funds to enforce boundaries, punishing some behaviors and girls, supporting others, and ignoring the rest (Reitsma-Street, 2004; Rosenberg & Garofalo, 1998). Border crossings by female youth, such as commission of crimes, can invoke anxiety, harsh judgments, and official interventions.

The low rates of participation of girls in criminal behaviors has led to theorizing about female crime and delinquency that, until the 1970s, largely overlooked girls' experiences. Some researchers (e.g., Cowie, Cowie, & Slater 1968) attempted to explain girls' criminal beh,avior as an aberration of "normal" femininity, or they proposed gender neutral explanations that decontextualized the complex reality of girls living in a gendered, racist, and unequal world (e.g., Hagan, Gillis, & Simpson, 1985). With the rise of feminism in academia and a concomitant groundswell in gender studies, more attention is being paid to the need for other explanations of girls' deviance, delinquency, and crime. But little, as yet, goes beyond the "add girls and stir" approach. Most research and practice is still largely caught up in comparing girls to boys and in attempting to adapt male-derived theories to work with females.

Some promising work has been done. Artz (1998), Chesney-Lind, and Pasko (2004) and Reitsma-Street (1998; 2004), among others, argue that crime by girls is not just a function of interactions within an established order. Illegal and other behaviors need to be understood as part of active struggles within a changing social order in which power and privilege are unequally distributed and frequently contested (e.g., Daly, 1997; Katz, 2000). These theorists suggest that to make sense of girls' crime, one must first understand girls' lives and the particular social conditions that prevail when girls become involved in criminal behaviors. To make sense of official crime statistics one must pay close attention to law, its construction and interpretation, and its application. The pervasive male standard about what is expected of female behavior needs to be examined and resisted in order to develop a fully delineated theory of girls' crime. Most of all, the voices and experiences of girls need to be put front and centre of the theories and practice.

In brief, responses to girls and crime need to be studied as a political project that can reveal how social order and gender inequity are established and how they are resisted. In the 21st century and in most of the previous century (Schissel, 1997), there have been fears about youth and the increase in crime and violence. Those fears flourish in times of economic insecurity. Law and order are often featured in debates on youth violence, popular culture, and political campaigns for elections. But crimes of youth do not just threaten people, property, or public order. They also threaten the apparent "natural order of things." This is especially true of crimes by girls, whose gender scripts do not include a "time to sow oats" or "to walk on the wild side."

Crimes by girls such as stealing, breaking into homes, not obeying probation orders, and hitting others scare people, even though the potential hurt and harm of these crimes are many times less than what can and does occur in automobile accidents, on worksites, or as a result of violence by adult family members. Crimes challenge the boundaries of what adults traditionally value as legal, feminine, productive, or valuable (Lees, 1997; Walkerdine et al., 2001).

RADICAL PRAGMATISM

An encompassing approach termed *radical pragmatism* emerges from research on girls and crime and from experience working with girls at risk and those convicted of breaking criminal laws. The features of radical pragmatism as presented in Table 1 are threefold. First, abolish the punitive practices and stereotypes that do not attend to girls' requirements of well-being. Second, expand what does work, including the effective, efficient community and school programs that prevent crime and promote well-being as well as differential treatment and compensatory, restorative initiatives for individual girls and groups. Third, politicize the need for equity and human rights by listening to what girls say they require to heal the hurts and prevent additional ones and by ensuring parity in funds and programs that build on what girls require.

TABLE 1. Radical Pragmatism

Abolish What Does Not Work:

- Eradicate the use of punitive policies and inhumane practices
- Stop indifference to girls' essential requirements for well-being
- Discontinue use of simplistic, stereotypical, binary ideas, theories and models

Expand What Does Work:

- Foster focused universal initiatives featuring strengths
- Increase compensatory interventions for damage from systemic inequities
- Promote differential treatment for girls and their networks

Politicize Equity and Human Rights:

- Listen to voices and experiences of girls and those who work with them
- Institute policies and practices to reverse systemic inequities
- Claim gender and racial parity in resources

ABOLISH WHAT DOES NOT WORK

The Scandavian criminologist Thomas Mathiesen (1974, 2000) is a leading proponent of the practice of abolishing inhuman, ineffective, and destructive policies and practices. He argues that competing ideas about crime and treatment need to be debated in expanding circles of those affected by crime. Demolishing inhumane, negative activities frees up space for the creation of flexible, voluntary and holistic practices (Brown & Hogg, 1985; West & Morris, 2000).

Mathiesen's writing and experience have been adopted by those working to abolish mail censorship in jails, reduce the number of custody beds, and stop violence campaigns (e.g., Dobash & Dobash, 1988). For example, politicians and professionals in Finland, as of 1975, have virtually abolished its youth prison system altogether. Only 10 youth under age 18 are imprisoned out of a population of five million (Mallea, 1999). In 1969, Jerome Miller in Massachusetts and, later, in Pennsylvania closed nearly all custody beds for youth, except for those secure units needed to treat highly disturbed youth who posed a danger to themselves and others. Individualized, flexible plans and sustained community interventions were developed by trained staff and volunteers to assist the majority of youth convicted of major and minor crimes. In follow-up research, Loughran (1997, p. 177) found that the Massachusetts community-based youth justice system, supported by several secure treatment programs, was cost-effective. Recidivism rates did not increase for 15 years after the custody centres were closed. Unfortunately, recent deep state cuts to community services accompanied by the pressure to increase youth sentences that are sweeping America undermine the effective abolitionist experiment in the Massachusetts youth justice system (Loughran, 1997; Platt, 2001).

Abolishing the use of punitive policies and discriminatory practices means reversing trends that dominate most of the American state youth justice systems and affect both girls and boys. These punitive trends permeate many aspects of the Canadian and British youth justice systems as well (Mallea, 1999; Platt, 2001). We must avoid discriminatory charging practices and custodial sentences. It means *not* charging 1 in 3 Canadian girls for administrative offences as is the practice in the 21st century youth courts. It means *not* managing Aboriginal girls in places thousands of miles from home and culture and radically changing correctional practices to reflect Aboriginal respect for spirit and land (Monture-Angus, 2000). It means closing correctional beds and the tough boot camps and removing the provisions regarding presumptive adult sentences for serious offences in the new Canadian *Youth Criminal Justice Act*.

Research demonstrates that discriminatory, harsh punishment is not effective, efficient, or humane (e.g., Green & Healy, 2003, p. 139). It destroys the development of positive relationships and community connections that are so essential to the well-being of girls. McCorkel's (2003) four-year evaluation and ethnographic study of the therapeutic community treatment for females convicted of using or selling drugs, for instance, demonstrates graphically that a punitive approach destroys what women consider valuable and humane. Extensive surveillance and intensive confrontations destroy trust, emotions, dignity, and the possibility of friendship and warmth among female inmates and staff.

Another feature of eliminating what does not work is to stop ignoring girls' requirements for survival, safety, and well-being. Girls cannot be responsible for the families, race, class, or neighbourhood into which they are born. At the end of the 20th century, 1 in 4 urban poor American high school students report they had seen someone killed, often someone they knew (Greene, 1993), as have all too many Aboriginal youth in Canada (Royal Commission on Aboriginal Peoples, 1993).

Whether they commit major or minor crimes, or none, girls are entitled to the requirements for well-being: economic survival, good education, adequate health services and housing, and safety from violence inside and outside homes. These requirements are necessary so girls do not trade the dangers and hurt of insecure, destructive, broken or violent families for dangerous streets and networks (Joe-Laidler & Hunt, 1997). Meeting girls' needs for survival implies abolishing the policies that are inequitable, minimalist, and discriminatory for girls including those in inner city schools, in jails, or on probation (e.g., Bloom, Owen, Deschenes, & Rosenbaum, 2002; Reitsma-Street 1999).

Research indicates that sustained quality education, apprenticeship, and housing programs that meet the essential requirements of girls at risk and those convicted of crimes are more effective in reducing recidivism and in increasing their well-being than the general, short-term counseling for primarily emotional, cognitive, or family problems (e.g., Bains & Alder, 1996; Chesney-Lind & Pasko, 2004) It also means abolishing policies that, for instance, prohibit girls (and boys) from access to social assistance. In the new 2002 *Employment and Assistance Law* of British Columbia there is a provision that prohibits young persons from applying for assistance unless they can prove two years of independent living or serious family abuse (Klein & Long, 2003).

The last feature of abolishing what does not work is to discontinue the use of stereotypes about girls and end incomplete, discriminatory assessments of their living situation. Girls live with the pervasive sentiments that they are not as important as boys while visible minority girls "can hang around" but black ones have to "get back, get back, get back" in the words of singer Faith Nolan. Katz (2000), for instance, documents how problematic life experiences (e.g., neighbourhood disorganization, physical abuse, alienation, and marginal peers) contribute to girls' involvement in delinquency and crime, but these strains are too often ignored.

In researching convicted girls transferred to the adult system, Gaarder and Belknap (2002) theorize about "blurred boundaries," especially the blurring that finds girls as both victims and offenders. Girls who may never have been allowed to be young are too often expected to act like responsible, rational adults. Pavlich (2001) argues that emphasizing only the pathology and deviance of individual girls overlooks their capacities and complexities and deflects attention away from systemic practices that maintain damaging and violent environments. Abolishing the binary, simplistic notions that pervades the "one size fits all" intervention frees up energy to develop the individualized, flexible interventions and healthy environments required by all.

EXPAND DIFFERENTIAL COMPENSATORY PRACTICES THAT WORK

Research and experience provides extensive guidance on interventions that do work. Greenwood, Model, Rydell and Chiesa (1998) conducted an evaluation of the cost-benefits of individual crime-prevention programs and incarceration. They found that early intervention programs such as early home visits combined with child day-care, parent training, and graduation incentive programs all contribute significant benefits to crime prevention. Of these three types of programs, graduation incentive programs produce the best cost-benefit ratio, largely because such programs are not very costly. These authors suggest that combining parent training with graduation incentives could reduce serious crime by 22%, and that early home visits and full-time day care for the first five years of life can reduce child abuse while also contributing to lower foster care costs and improved school performance.

Universal initiatives that support the strengths and well-being of all girls need to be fostered. Practices and social policies focus specifically on one or more of the well-being requirements and are available and delivered to all the children and youth in a class, school, neigbourhood, community, cultural group, province, state, or nation. This universal approach is different than professionals targeting only "high risk" girls in a classroom or "multiproblem" families in a neighbourhood. Instead, all are eligible and invited to use the teen centre, quality childcare, housing, food, health insurance and services, education, violence prevention programs, and community resource centres (Reitsma-Street & Neysmith, 2000). For example, whole school programs that involve teachers, students, and parents working together to raise the level of social consciousness in schools and communities have proven to be the most effective violence prevention approach (see Shariff, 2000).

In a longitudinal study of 11 London high schools, Rutter (1980) found that girls and boys with lower achievement and a higher propensity for behaviour problems in Grade 9 did better on academic, social, and behaviour measures over four years in good high schools than did smarter students in schools with less positive environments. The good or positive schools had strong scholastic expectations, high relationship support, and cohesive, democratic governance structures that included students in making discipline codes. Whether using the "capacity building," "holistic intervention," or a "wellness paradigm"–the orientation to well-being of all, not just the targeted few–abolishes the limited focus on negative problem behaviors, criminal thinking, or mental illness of girls. For example, Hartwig and Myers (2003) demonstrate the use of the wellness paradigm in individual and group practice to address the girls' requirements for spirituality, self-direction, work and leisure, friendship, and physical health.

Schools are important sites to promote the exercise of democratic values such as debate and confrontation of inequality and to discourage cultures that contribute to aggressive and violent behaviour (Öhrn, 2001). Teachers deconstruct gender with students and debate how the dominant culture emphasizes the importance of achieving power and status through competition (Connell, 1996). There are a number of ways teachers can do this. Teachers can talk openly about the "boy code" and insist that boys do not have to be tough and dominant. The boy code devalues relationships, emotions, and femininity (Pollack, 1998). Teachers and schools can also work to prevent violence and racism by recognizing that social exclusion and discrimination is damaging to children and is often at the root of much of the physical violence and racist attacks that occur in schools (Birkinshaw & Eslea, 1998; Öhrn, 2001). By paying attention to their own propensity to evaluate students' behaviour more harshly when it does not conform to gender stereotypes, teachers can learn to evaluate students' behaviour in new ways. By recognizing that beliefs about boys needing to be sufficiently "masculine" and girls needing to be sufficiently "feminine" contribute to the perpetuation of sexual harassment–63% of which is committed by same sex peers–teachers can help to reduce this form of aggression among students (Fineran, 2002).

The other aspects of expanding what works are related but distinct. There is the systematic attention to compensatory interventions to repair systemic inequities that damage individuals and groups. These types of interventions do not assume the social order is good or needs to be maintained as there is systemic injustice that Aboriginal, poor, disabled girls face every day. In her study of Latina teenagers living in New York City, Madriz (1997) found all had been victims of violence and crimes, with the girls feeling like they had "two strikes" against them by being female and Latina. Neither girls nor boys saw the police or justice officials as helpful and they resented feeling they did not belong and lived in "a constant state of apprehension for what can happen to them, but especially for what can happen to family members, especially mothers, sisters and brothers" (p. 52).

Third world and feminist scholars argue that crimes are not only interactions within an established order but part of active struggles within a social order in which privileges are unequally distributed and frequently contested (Connell, 1987; Hall, Jefferson, & Critchers, 1978). Aboriginal girls and girls of colour speak of their anger, fear, and desire to push back against a social order in which privileges are unequally distributed and frequently contested (Monture-Angus, 2000). Thus, girls and their families struggle not just to become functional but struggle to overcome systemic inequities that create barriers to functional development. They seek redress for destruction. These struggles against injustice are themselves constrained by sets of acceptable ideas about what is a "good girl," "justice," and a "productive citizen," and the unequal distribution of resources to income, education, job opportunities, and birth control.

Compensatory and restorative interventions take seriously the stressors and damage that racism, cultural deprivation, chronic violence, abuse, alcohol abuse, mental and physical illness, and inadequate schooling inflict on a girl and her support systems. The family, restorative, and integrated case conferencing provisions in the new Canadian *Youth Criminal Justice Act* may provide opportunities for compensatory interventions if the community is actively involved. Unfortunately there are no mandatory provisions in the law to provide resources for conferencing or implementation of their recommendations (Hillian, Reitsma-Street, & Hackler, 2004).

Compensatory interventions can address the offending patterns associated with different times of the day or month or the different spaces and environments in neighbourhoods, schools, and families, or even the different stages in the lives of youth and their peer groups. For example, Thurman, Giacomazzi, Reisig, and Mueller (1996) showed that providing youth at risk with attractive and safe alternative activities in their neighbourhoods and, at times, particularly late at night, when they would normally be on the streets, helped to reduce crime considerably. Longitudinal studies of sustained family support and Head Start programs for all children and families in poor neighbourhoods indicate that delinquency rates are lower and well-being higher than in comparable neighbourhoods without these programs (Campbell, Muncer, & Bibel, 1998; Pancer et al., 2003; Schwartz & Au Claire, 1995; Smith & Stern, 1997).

Besides compensatory reparations, classification and differential treatment has long aided the efficient management and effective treatment of girls, including those convicted of crimes (Palmer, 1995). The research demonstrates that youth learn more and recidivate less when their diverse learning styles, cognitive abilities, and emotional maturity are responded to in a systematic way whether in the organization of the correctional environment or style of probation worker supervision (e.g., Hunt & Hardt, 1965; Reitsma-Street & Leschied, 1988; Warren, 1971). For instance, Stoppard and Henri (1987) designed two versions of assertiveness training for girls and women who varied in their cognitive capacity to tolerate ambiguity, uncertainty, and authority. The high structure version matched those whose cognitive capacity required fixed sequences of activities, ready-made rules, firm and enthusiastic leadership, and generous support for success.

In the low structure approach, group discussions were facilitated by a leader. Thirty-six women were randomly assigned to 8 hours of assertiveness training over 4 weeks, and those whose cognitive style matched the treatment approach learned more about assertiveness than those in the approach that did not match their style of learning. Thus far, results for differential treatment have been promising, especially when sustained over time as in the long term coordinated multi-systemic therapy for serious juvenile offenders and their families (Henggeler, Melton, & Smith, 1992) and in the intense thoughtful approaches to convicted girls living with serious mental illness, trauma from abuse, and heavy substance use (Trupin et al., 1999).

POLITICIZE EQUITY AND HUMAN RIGHTS

The last component of the radical pragmatism approach to girls and crime is to politicize equity and inequities and to foster attention to human rights. This means laws and policies are written to promote gender and racial equity and public resources are made available to implement those laws and policies. In recent history, girls had been treated more paternalistically and harshly than boys, particularly for minor illegal, status, or unfeminine behaviors (Geller, 1987; Parent, 1986; Reitsma-Street, 1989). Some argue that gender discrimination may no longer be so obvious in Canada or elsewhere (De Como, 1998; Kowalski & Caputo, 2001). Under the 1984 *Young Offenders Act*, for example, status offences were eliminated.

Yet the reduction of gender discriminatory practices may be illusory. Girls of Aboriginal or visible minority status remain particularly vulnerable to discriminatory treatment (Chesney-Lind & Pasko, 2004; Fisher & Janti, 2000). As mentioned previously, 1 in 3 girls in youth court were charged with administrative offences in 2000. There are no comparable offenses for adults, yet these administrative offenses are not minor in their consequences for girls. More Canadian girls are sentenced to custody on administrative charges than for either minor or major violent crimes (Reitsma-Street, 1999). In one study, breaches of court orders comprised 45% of the girls' current charges and 69% of previous ones (Corrado, Odgers, & Cohen, 2000). There are additional provisions in the new Act that may be used to charge youth who have breached post custody conditions. Aboriginal girls continue to be disportionately charged and sentenced to custody, making up one-third to one-half of custody populations in some provinces (Corrado, Odgers, & Cohen, 2000).

Thus, the radical pragmatism approach to girls and crime means strategic attention to rights and resources that promote gender and racial equity. One aspect of this press for equity and rights is captured in the common phrase "listening to girls' voices" (Nicholson & Artz, 2003; Reitsma-Street & Offord, 1991; Rosenberg & Garofalo, 1998; Walkerdine et al., 2001). Girls in the cultural Riot Grrrl movement, for example, speak graphically and holistically of what is wrong and what is desired. For instance one states:

> The problem is obvious: the solution is probably more simple than we admit. Why don't we admit it? The air is bad, the sky is bad: the water is bad. There's inequality. We shouldn't have to live with it. (Rosenberg & Garofalo, 1998, p. 829)

There are important policy implications to listening to what youth in the new peace movement are saying and doing: cessation of violence on the streets, negotiating truces and cease-fires among warring street organizations, and building neighbourhood recreation (Childs, 1997). Youth activists inside and outside the justice system speak clearly about rights, including the right to have safe and healthy spaces in homes, schools, libraries, and and the right to redress from racism and destruction of pride, community, and heritage (Green & Healy, 2003; Meucci & Redmon, 1997; Schaffner, Schick, & Stein, 1997). The political implication of listening means development of policies and practices that incorporate what girls say they want and need: ending violence in the streets and in homes, a good education and job, and supporting the work of building relationships and caring for others.

Besides implementing policies that respond to what girls say they require to prevent problems and reduce recidivism, it is necessary to examine how particular interests are served by discrimination and injustice. Who benefits from the increase in charging girls with administrative offenses and overcrowding in jails? Why do governments refuse to make reparations for past abuses in Aboriginal residential schools and correctional centres such as the Ontario Grandview Training School for girls (Kershaw & Lasovich, 1991)? Interventions are required that strategically dismantle inequitable policies and compensate for the destruction of rights.

Politicizing rights and equity means, above all, an insistence that funding and legislative resources for girls in the justice system are proportionate to their numbers and requirements for well-being (Bloom, Owen, Deschenes, & Rosenbaum, 2002; Green & Healy, 2003). This means parity in access to apprenticeship training, English as a second language, housing, sports programs, and post-secondary education. The disproportionate and lower levels of funding for girls than boys must be abolished, such as the fact that only 10% of funds in the San Francisco justice and welfare system were allocated to girls although they make up 25 percent of the total (Schaffner, Shick, & Stein, 1997, p. 205).

Politicizing equity would mean that at least one-fifth of Canadian youth justice funds and resources are explicitly tied to girls and their well-being and proportionately more to Aboriginal and Métis girls. But, these funds should not be used to pay for longer custody sentences or more courts and police officers. Rather, I support the recommendation of the Canadian parliamentary committee and the Department of Justice that 80% federal and provincial correctional funding be for community, compensatory, differential initiatives, the reverse of the current situation where most of the money goes into custody facilities and staff (Department of Justice, 1998; House of Commons, 1997).

CONCLUDING COMMENTS

Girls engage in antisocial, deviant, and criminal behavior, but their participation is sporadic and episodic; rarely do they develop specialties. Charges against young females for serious crimes of violence has remained remarkably constant for decades in Canada and elsewhere, while official charges for administrative offences and technical violations have increased dramatically, making up 1 in 3 charges by 2000. Girls' minimal, episodic involvement in crime has led to an approach to theorizing about female crime and delinquency that, until the 1970s, largely overlooked girls' experiences. Most research and practice were also caught up in comparing girls to boys and in attempting to adapt male-derived theories to work with females.

Crime and responses to girls and crime need to be studied as a political project, that is, an examination of how social order and gender inequity are established, by whom and how and, then, how it is resisted, by whom and how. With the abolitionist, compensatory, and political aspects of a radically pragmatic approach to working with girls, policy-makers and practitioners make two commitments. They commit to recognize the complex intersections of the gendered, racist world in which girls live. They also commit to building the dignified world girls desire.

REFERENCES

Artz, S. (1998). *Sex, power and the violent school girl.* Toronto, ON: Trifolium.

Artz, S., Riecken, T., MacIntyre, B., Lam, E., & Maczewski, M. (1999). A community-based violence prevention project, University of Victoria and School District 62, B.C. Health Research Foundation final report.

Bains, M., & Alder, C. (1996). Are girls more difficult to work with? Youth workers' perspectives in juvenile justice and related areas. *Crime & Delinquency, 42*(3), 467-485.

Birkinshaw, S., & Eslea, M. (1998). Teachers' attitudes and actions toward boy v. girl and girl v. boy bullying. Paper presented at the Annual Conference of the Developmental Section of the British Psychological Society, Lancaster University, September, 1998.

Bloom, B., Owen, B., Deschenes, E. P., & Rosenbaum, J. (2002). Improving juvenile justice for females: A statewide assessment in California. *Crime and Delinquency, 48*(4), 526-552.

Brown, D., & Hogg, R. (1985). Abolition reconsidered: Issues and problems. *Australian Journal of Law and Society, 2*(2), 56-75.

Browne, M. (2003). Survey says being young can hurt. Victoria News, Dec 3, 2003, p. 4.

Cain, M. (Ed.) (1989). *Growing up good: Policing the behaviour of girls in Europe.* London, Newbury Park, New Delhi: Sage.

Carrington, P. (1999). Trends in youth crime in Canada 1977-1996. *Canadian Journal of Criminology, 41*(1), 1-32.

Campbell, A., Muncer, S., & Bibel, D. (1998). Female-female criminal assault: An evolutionary perspective. *Journal of Research in Crime and Delinquency, 35*, 413-428.

Chesney-Lind, M., & Okamoto, S. (2001). Gender matters: Patterns in girl's delinquency and gender responsive programming. *Journal of Forensic Psychology Practice, 1*(3), 1-28.

Chesney-Lind, M., & Pasko, L. (Eds.) (2004). *Girls, women and crime: Selected readings.* Thousand Oaks, CA: Sage.

Childs, J. B. (1997). The new Youth Peace Movement: Creating broad strategies for community renaissance in the United States. *Social Justice, 24*(4), 247-257.

Connell, R. W. (1987). *Gender and power.* Cambridge, MA: Polity Press.

Connell, R. W. (1996). Teaching the boys: New research on masculinity, and gender strategies for schools. *Teachers College Record, 98*(2), 207-235.

Corrado, R., Odgers, C., & Cohen, I. (2000, April). The incarceration of female young offenders: Protection for whom? *Canadian Journal of Criminology,* 189-207.

Cowie, J., Cowie, V., & Slater, E. (1968). *Delinquency in girls.* London: Heinemann.

Daly, K. (1997). Different ways of conceptualizing sex/gender in feminist theory and their implications for criminology. *Theoretical Criminology, 1*(1), 25-51.

De Como, R. E. (1998). Estimating the prevalence of juvenile custody by race and gender. *Crime & Delinquency, 44*(4), 489-506.

Department of Justice Canada (1998). *A strategy for the renewal of youth justice.* Ottawa, ON: Department of Justice Canada.

Dobash, R. E., & Dobash, R. (Eds.) (1988). *Rethinking violence against women.* Thousand Oaks, CA: Sage.

Doob, A., & Sprott, J. (1998). Is the "quality" of youth violence becoming more serious? *Canadian Journal of Criminology, 40,* 185-194.

Estrada, F. (2001). Juvenile violence as a social problem: Trends, media attention and societal response. *British Journal of Criminology, 41,* 639-655.

Fineran, S. (2002). Sexual harassment between same-sex peers: Intersection of mental health, homophobia, and sexual violence in schools. *Social Work, 47*(1), 65-74.

Fisher, L., & Jantti, H. (2000). Aboriginal youth and the youth justice system. In J. Winterdyk (Ed.), *Issues and perspectives on young offenders in Canada.* 2nd ed. Toronto: Harcourt.

Gaarder, E., & Belknap, J. (2002). Tenuous borders: Girls transferred to adult court. *Criminolgy, 40*(3), 481-517.

Geller, G. (1987). Young women in conflict with the law. In E. Adelberg & C. Currie (Eds.), *Too few to count.* Vancouver, BC: Press Gang.

Green, R., & Healy, K. (2003). *Tough on kids: Rethinking approaches to youth justice.* Saskatoon, SK: Purich.

Greene, M. B. (1993). Chronic exposure to violence and poverty: Interventions that work for youth. *Crime and Delinquency, 39*(1), 106-124.

Greenwood, P., Model, K., Rydell, C., & Chiesa, J. (1998). *Diverting children from a life of crime: Measuring costs and benefits.* Oakland, CA: RAND Criminal Justice.

Hagan, J., Gillis, A., & Simpson, J. (1985). The class structure of delinquency: Toward a power control theory of common delinquent behavior. *American Journal of Sociology, 90,* 1151-1178.

Hagan, J., & McCarthy, B. (1997). *Mean streets: Youth crime and homelessness.* Cambridge, NY: Cambridge University Press.

Hall, S., Jefferson, T., & Critchers, M. (1978). *Policing the crisis: Mugging, the state, and law and order.* London: Macmillan.

Hartwig, J., & Myers, J. E. (2003). A different approach: Applying a wellness paradigm to adolescent female delinquents and offenders. *Journal of Mental Health Counseling, 5*(1), 57-75.

Henggler, S. W., Melton, G. B., & Smith, L. D. (1992). Family preservation using multisystemic therapy: An effective alternative to incarcerating serious juvenile offenders. *Journal of Consulting and Clinical Psychology, 60*(6), 953-961.

Hillian, D., Reitsma-Street, M., & Hackler, J. (2004). Conferencing in the Youth Criminal Justice Act of Canada: Policy developments in British Columbia. *Canadian Journal of Criminology & Criminal Justice, 46*, 344-366.

House of Commons (1997). *Renewing youth justice.* 13th Report of the Standing Committee on Justice and Legal Affairs, Shaughnessy Cohen, Chair. Ottawa, ON: Queen's Printer.

Hunt, D. E., & Hardt, R. H. (1965). Developmental stage, delinquency, and differential treatment. *Journal of Research in Crime and Delinquency, 2*, 20-31.

Joe-Laidler, K., & Hunt, G. (1997). Violence and social organization in female gangs. *Social Justice, 24*, 148-169.

Katz, R. (2000). Explaining girl's and women's crime and desistance in the context of their victimization experiences. *Violence Against Women, 6*(6), 633-660.

Kershaw, A., & Lasovich, M. (1991). *Rock-a-bye baby: A death behind bars.* Toronto, ON: McClelland & Stewart.

Klein, S., & Long, A. (2003). *A bad time to be poor: An analysis of British Columbia's new welfare policies.* Vancouver: Canadian Centre for Policy Alternatives-BC Office & Social Planning and Research Council.

Kowalski, M., & Caputo, T. (2001). Recidivism in youth court: An examination of the impact of age, gender, and prior record. In T. Fleming, P. O'Reilly, & B. Clark (Eds.), *Youth injustice: Canadian perspectives* (2nd ed.) (pp. 483-510). Toronto, ON: Canadian Scholars' Press.

Lees, S. (1997). *Ruling passions: Sexual violence, reputation and the law.* Buckingham: Open University Press.

Loughran, E. J. (1997). The Massachusetts experience: A historical review of reform in the Department of Youth Services. *Social Justice 24*(4), 170-186.

Madriz, E. (1997). Latina teenagers: Victimization, identity, and fear of crime. *Social Justice, 24*(4), 39-55.

Mallea, P. (1999). *Getting tough on kids: Young offenders and the "law and order" agenda.* Winnipeg, MB: Canadian Centre for Policy Alternatives.

Marcus, R. F. (1999). A gender-linked exploratory factor analysis of antisocial behaviour in young adolescents. *Adolescence, 34*(133), 33-46.

Mathiesen, T. (1974). *The politics of abolition.* Oslo, Universitetsforlaget, Martin Robertson.

Mathiesen, T. (2000). Towards the 21st century: Abolition–an impossible dream? In W. B. G. West & R. Morris (Eds.), *The case for penal abolition* (pp. 33-56). Toronto, ON: Canadian Scholars' Press.

McCorkel, J. A. (2003). Embodied surveillance and the gendering of punishment. *Journal of Contemporary Ethnography, 32*(1) 41-76.

Meucci, S., & Redmon, J. (1997). Safe spaces: California children enter a policy debate. *Social Justice, 24*(3), 139-151.

Monture-Angus, P. (2000). Aboriginal women and correctional practice. In K. Hannah-Moffat & M. Shaw (Eds.), *An ideal prison? Critical essays on women's imprisonment in Canada* (pp. 52-60). Halifax, NS: Fernwood.

Moretti, M., Odgers, C., & Jackson, M. (Eds.) (2004). *Girls and aggression: Contributing factors and intervention principles*. Boston, MA: Kluwer.

Nicholson, D., & Artz, S. (2003). Preventing youthful offending: Where do we go from here? *Relational Child and Youth Care Practice, 16*(4), 32-46.

Öhrn, E. (2001). Marginalization of democratic values: A gendered practice of schooling? *International Journal of Inclusive Education, 5*(2/3), 319-328.

Palmer, T. (1995). Programmatic and nonprogrammatic aspects of successful intervention. *Crime & Delinquency, 41*(1), 100-131.

Pancer, M., Nelson, G., Dearing, B., Dearing, S., Hayward, K., & Peters, R. Dev. (2003). Promoting wellness in children and families through community-based interventions: The Highfield Community Enrichment Project (Better Beginnings, Better Futures). In K. Kufeldt & B. McKenzie (Eds.), *Child welfare: Connecting research, policy, and practice*. Waterloo, ON: Wifrid Laurier University Press.

Parent, C. (1986). Actualitès et bibliographies: La protection chevalresque ou les representations masculines du traitement des femmes dans la justice pénale. *Déviance et Société, 10*(2), 147-175.

Pavlich, G. (2001). Critical genres and radical criminology in Britain. *British Journal of Criminology, 41*, 150-167.

Platt, A. (2001). Social insecurity: The transformation of American criminal justice, 1965-2000. *Social Justice, 28*(1), 138-154.

Pollack, W. (1998). *Real boys: Rescuing our sons from the myths of boyhood*. New York: Henry Holt.

Reitsma-Street, M. (1989). More control than care: A critique of historical and contemporary laws for delinquency and neglect of children in Ontario. *Canadian Journal. of Women and the Law, 3*(2), 510-530.

Reitsma-Street, M. (1998). Still girls learn to care; girls policed to care. In C. Baines, P. Evans, & S. Neysmith (Eds.), *Women's caring: Social policy in Canada* (Rev. Edition) (pp. 87-113). Toronto, ON: Oxford University Press.

Reitsma-Street, M. (1999). Justice for Canadian girls: A 1990s update. *Canadian Journal of Criminology, 41*(4), 335-363.

Reitsma-Street, M. (2004). Connecting policies, girls, and violence. In M. Moretti, C. Odgers, & M. Jackson (Eds.), *Girls and aggression: Contributing factors and intervention principles* (pp. 115-130). Boston, MA: Kluwer.

Reitsma-Street, M., & Leschied, A. W. (1988). The conceptual-level matching model in corrections. *Criminal Justice and Behavior, 15*(1), 92-108.

Reitsma-Street, M. & Neysmith, S. (2000). Restructuring and community work: The case of community resource centres for families in poor urban neighbourhoods. In S. Neysmith (Eds.), *Restructuring caring labour: Discourse, state practice, and everyday life* (pp. 142-163). Toronto, ON: Oxford University Press.

Reitsma-Street, M., & Offord, D. R. (1991). Girl delinquents and their sisters: A challenge for practice. *Canadian Social Work Review, 8*(1), 11-27.

Reitsma-Street, M., Artz, S., & Nicholson (in press). Canadian girls and crime in the twenty-first century. In J. Winterdyk (Ed.), *Issues and perspectives on young offenders in Canada* (3rd edition). Nelson.

Rosenberg, J., & Garofalo, G. (1998). Riot grrrl: Revolutions from within. *Signs, 23*(3), 809-842.

Royal Commission on Aboriginal Peoples (1993). *Aboriginal peoples and the justice system*. Ottawa, ON: Minister of Supplies and Services Canada.

Rutter, M. (1980). School influences on children's behavior and development. *Pediatrics, 65*(2), 208-220.

Schaffner, L., Shick, S., & Stein, N. (1997). Changing policy in San Francisco: Girls in the juvenile justice system. *Social Justice, 24*(4), 187-211.

Schissel, B. (1997). Youth crime, moral panics, and the news: The conspiracy against the marginalized in Canada. *Social Justice, 24*(2), 187-211.

Schwartz, I. M., & Au Claire, P. (Eds.). (1995). *Home-based services for troubled children*. Lincoln, NE: University of Nebraska Press.

Shariff, S. (2000). *Identifying successful school and community programs for youth: An evaluation rubric and compendium of sources*. Youth Justice Education Partnerships. Retrieved April 20, 2003, from *http://www.extension.ualberta.ca/youthjustice/rubric.doc*

Smith, C., & Stern, S. (1997, September). Delinquency and antisocial behaviour: A review of family processes and intervention research. *Social Service Review*, 383-420.

Statistics Canada (2002). *Adults and youths charged by sex using Uniform Crime Reporting Survey and Estimates of Population by age and sex for Canada*. CANSIM II Series V12442. Ottawa, Ontario: Author.

Stoppard, J. M., & Henri, G. S. (1987). Conceptual level matching and effects of assertiveness training. *Journal of Counseling Psychology, 34*, 55-61.

Thurman, Q. C., Giacomazzi, A. L., Reisig, M. D., & Mueller, D. G. (1996). Community-based gang prevention and intervention: An evaluation of a neutral zone. *Crime & Delinquency, 42*(2), 279-295.

Trupin, E., Stewart, D., Boesky, L., McClurg, B., Beach, B., Hormann, S., & Baltrusis, R. (1999, February). *Evaluation of a dialectical behavior therapy with incarcerated female juvenile offenders*. Paper presented at the 11th annual research conference, A System of Care for Children's Mental Health: Expanding the Research Base. Tampa, FL.

Walkerdine, V., Lucey, H., & Melody, J. (2001). *Growing up girl: Psychosocial explorations of gender and class*. Houndmills, Basingstoke, Hampshire: Palgrave.

Warren, M. Q. (1971). Classification of offenders as an aid to efficient management and effective treatment. *Journal of Criminal Law, Criminology, & Police Science, 62*(2), 239-258.

West, W. B. G., & Morris, R. (Eds.) (2000). *The case for penal abolition*. Toronto, ON: Canadian Scholars' Press.

Williams, L. S. (2002). Trying on gender, gender regimes, and the process of becoming women. *Gender and Society, 16*(1), 29-52.

Index

BOOK ORDER FORM!

Order a copy of this book with this form or online at:
http://www.HaworthPress.com/store/product.asp?sku=5652

Working Relationally with Girls
Complex Lives/Complex Identities

_____ in softbound at $22.95 ISBN-13: 978-0-7890-2993-5 / ISBN-10: 0-7890-2993-6.
_____ in hardbound at $34.95 ISBN-13: 978-0-7890-2992-8 / ISBN-10: 0-7890-2992-8.

COST OF BOOKS _____

POSTAGE & HANDLING _____
US: $4.00 for first book & $1.50
for each additional book.
Outside US: $5.00 for first book
& $2.00 for each additional book.

SUBTOTAL _____

In Canada: add 7% GST. _____

STATE TAX _____
CA, IL, IN, MN, NJ, NY, OH, PA & SD residents
please add appropriate local sales tax.

FINAL TOTAL _____
If paying in Canadian funds, convert
using the current exchange rate,
UNESCO coupons welcome.

❑ **BILL ME LATER:**
Bill-me option is good on US/Canada/
Mexico orders only; not good to jobbers,
wholesalers, or subscription agencies.

❑ **Signature** _____

❑ **Payment Enclosed: $** _____

❑ **PLEASE CHARGE TO MY CREDIT CARD:**

❑ Visa ❑ MasterCard ❑ AmEx ❑ Discover
❑ Diner's Club ❑ Eurocard ❑ JCB

Account # _____

Exp Date _____

Signature _____
(Prices in US dollars and subject to change without notice.)

PLEASE PRINT ALL INFORMATION OR ATTACH YOUR BUSINESS CARD

Name

Address

City   State/Province   Zip/Postal Code

Country

Tel   Fax

E-Mail

May we use your e-mail address for confirmations and other types of information? ❑ Yes ❑ No We appreciate receiving
your e-mail address. Haworth would like to e-mail special discount offers to you, as a preferred customer.
We will never share, rent, or exchange your e-mail address. We regard such actions as an invasion of your privacy.

Order from your **local bookstore** or directly from
The Haworth Press, Inc. 10 Alice Street, Binghamton, New York 13904-1580 • USA
Call our toll-free number (1-800-429-6784) / Outside US/Canada: (607) 722-5857
Fax: 1-800-895-0582 / Outside US/Canada: (607) 771-0012
E-mail your order to us: orders@HaworthPress.com

For orders outside US and Canada, you may wish to order through your local
sales representative, distributor, or bookseller.
For information, see http://HaworthPress.com/distributors

(Discounts are available for individual orders in US and Canada only, not booksellers/distributors.)

Please photocopy this form for your personal use.
www.HaworthPress.com

BOF05